Anonymous

Circular requiring tax collectors to retain and pay over all the coin collected

Anonymous

Circular requiring tax collectors to retain and pay over all the coin collected

ISBN/EAN: 9783337714970

Printed in Europe, USA, Canada, Australia, Japan

Cover: Foto ©ninafisch / pixelio.de

More available books at **www.hansebooks.com**

CIRCULAR REQUIRING TAX COLLECTORS TO RETAIN AND PAY OVER ALL THE COIN COLLECTED.

CONFEDERATE STATES OF AMERICA,
TREASURY DEPARTMENT,
RICHMOND, January 10, 1862.

SIR: The law requires that the war taxes shall be paid in coin or Treasury Notes. For obvious reasons, you will require your sub-collectors to retain and pay over to you all the specie collected and forbid them to exchange any coin thus collected for Treasury Notes. Any regulation or plan you may adopt calculated to secure this object will receive the approbation of this Department.

Very respectfully,

(Signed.) C. G. MEMMINGER,
Secretary of Treasury.

REGULATIONS IN REFERENCE TO THE COMPENSATION OF SUB-COLLECTORS, IN CERTAIN CASES.

Confederate States of America,
Treasury Department,
Richmond, May 13, 1862.

Congress having passed an Act to authorize the Secretary of the Treasury to pay District Collectors in certain cases, the following regulations for the establishment of their claims, under the Act, must be observed.

The Secretary, being authorized by the Act, to pay the several District Collectors of the War Tax, in those States that have assumed the payment of the War Tax, an amount not to exceed the sum of one hundred dollars, each Collector in such States, who shall have given bond and discharged the duties required by law, shall make out an account stated against the Confederate States, for compensation not to exceed the sum, one hundred dollars, to which account he shall attach his name. The account shall state the services performed, and the Chief Collector of his State shall certify in writing, upon said account, that said Collector has given bond and performed to his satisfaction the duties required of him by law, after which the account shall be transmitted to the Treasury Department for examination and settlement.

The assessors in each State will render their accounts to the Chief Collector, who shall certify the same to the Treasury Department, whereupon, after being duly audited, Treasury drafts for each claim will be forwarded to the Chief Collector to be delivered to the several assessors.

C. G. MEMMINGER,
Secretary of Treasury.

No. 34.] AN ACT

To authorize the Secretary of the Treasury to pay District Collectors in certain cases.

SECTION 1. *The Congress of the Confederate States of America do enact,* That the Secretary of the Treasury be, and he is hereby authorized to pay a part of the salaries of the several District Collectors of the War Tax, authorized by the act entitled "an act to authorize the issue of Treasury notes, and to provide a War Tax for their redemption," approved August 19th, 1861, in those states which have assumed the payment of said tax: *Provided,* that in no case shall the amount so paid to each Collector exceed the sum of one hundred dollars: And *Provided further,* the Secretary of the Treasury shall be satisfied that said Collector gave bond and rendered services as required by said act, previous to the assumption of said tax by the respective States, equal in value to the sum to be paid.

APPROVED April 11, 1862.

CIRCULAR IN REFERENCE TO THE QUALIFICATION OF TAX COLLECTORS.

CONFEDERATE STATES OF AMERICA,
TREASURY DEPARTMENT,
RICHMOND, October 12, 1862.

SIR: On page 2 of the War Tax Instructions, it is required that "each tax collector shall take the usual oath of office, and shall give bond for the faithful performance of the duties of his office, with sufficient sureties, in a sum sufficient to cover the presumptive amount of taxes which he will collect until that sum shall reach $ 25,000." To facilitate the speedy qualification of tax collectors, the sufficiency of their sureties may be certified by any Judge of the Confederate District Courts or Judge of a State Court, or Presiding Justice of any County Court, and the oath may be administered by any Acting Justice of the Peace. The bond must be attested by two or more credible witnesses, and when complete, must be sent to the chief collector and by him registered, and then sent to the Treasury Department.

Very respectfully,

(Signed,) C. G. MEMMINGER,
Secretary of Treasury.

Gray

TAX AND ASSESSMENT ACTS,

AND AMENDMENTS.

January & February 1864.

THE TAX ACT OF 24th APRIL 1863, AS AMENDED

February 17. 1864. —

AN ACT to amend an Act entitled "An Act to lay taxes for the common defence and carry on the Government of the Confederate States," approved April 24th, 1863.

The Congress of the Confederate States of America do enact, That an Act entitled "An Act to lay taxes for the common defence, and carry on the Government of the Confederate States," approved April 24, 1863, be and the same is hereby amended, so as to read as follows:

REGISTRATION OF BUSINESS.

Business to be registered within sixty days after passage of act, and 1st January in each year thereafter.

SEC. 1. Every person engaged or intending to engage in any business named in the fourth section of this act, shall within sixty days after the passage of this act, or at the time of beginning business, and on the first day of January in each year thereafter, register with the district collector, in such form as the commissioner of taxes shall prescribe, a true account of the name and residence of each person, firm, or corporation engaged or interested in the business, with a statement of the time for which, and the place and manner in which the same is to be conducted, and of all other facts going to ascertain the amount of tax upon such business for the past or the future, according to the provisions of this act. At the time of such registry, there shall be paid to the collector the specific tax for the year, ending on the next thirty-first of December, and such other tax as may be due upon sales or receipts in such business, at the time of such registry, as herein provided; and the collector shall give to the person making such registry a copy thereof, with a receipt for the amount of tax then paid.

Specific tax paid at time of registry.

SEC. 2. That any person failing to make the registry, and to pay the tax required by the preceding section, shall in addition to all other taxes upon his business imposed by this act, pay double the amount of the specific tax on such business, and a like sum for every thirty days of such failure.

Defaulters pay double tax.

SEC. 3. That except where herein otherwise provided, there shall be a separate registry and tax for each business mentioned in the fourth section of this act, and for each place of conducting the same, but no tax shall be required for the mere storage of goods at a place other than

Separate registry to be kept.

the registered place of business. Upon every change in the place of conducting a registered business, there shall be a new registry, but no additional tax shall be required. Upon the death of any person conducting a business registered and taxed as herein required, or upon the transfer of the business to another, the business shall not be subjected to any additional tax, but there shall be a new registry in the name of the person authorized by law to continue the business.

In case of death or change of place new registry to be made.

BANKERS, AUCTIONEERS, DEALERS, ETC.

SEC. 4. That upon each trade, business or occupation hereinafter named, the following taxes shall be levied and paid for the year, ending on the thirty-first of December, eighteen hundred and sixty-three, and for each and every year thereafter, viz:

Tax paid for year ending 31st December.

I. Bankers shall pay five hundred dollars. Every person shall be deemed a banker within the meaning of this act who keeps a place of business where credits are opened in favor of any person, firm or corporation, by the deposit or collection of money or currency, and by whom the same or any part thereof shall be paid out or remitted upon the draft, check or order of such creditor; but not to include any bank legally authorized to issue notes as circulation, nor agents for the sale of merchandize for account of producers or manufacturers.

Bankers $500.

Banks of issue not included.

II. Auctioneers shall pay fifty dollars and two and a half per centum on the gross amount of sales made: *Provided however*, That on all sales at auction of stock or securities for money, the tax shall be one fourth of one per centum on the gross amount of sales. Every person shall be deemed an auctioneer, within the meaning of this act, whose occupation it is to offer property for sale to the highest or best bidder at public outcry. The tax upon the auctioneers shall be deemed a tax upon the personal privilege, to be paid by each individual engaged in the business, and without regard to the place at which the same is conducted. No tax shall be required upon auction sales made for dealers in a business registered and taxed, and at their place of business, or upon official sales at auction, made by judicial or executive officers, or by personal representatives, guardians or committees.

Auctioneers $50 and two and a half per cent. on gross sales, one fourth of one per cent. on stock.

No tax on persons registered and taxed.

III. Wholesale dealers in liquors of any and every description, including distilled spirits, fermented liquors, and wines of all kinds, shall pay two hundred dollars, and five per centum on the gross amount of sales made. Every person, other than the distiller or brewer, who shall sell or offer for sale, any such liquors or wines, in quantities of more than three gallons at one time, to the same purchaser, shall be regarded as a wholesale dealer in liquors, within the meaning of this act. All persons who shall sell, or offer for sale, any such liquors or wines, in quantities less than three gallons at one time to the same person, shall be regarded as a retail dealer in liquors.

Wholesale dealers in liquors, $200 and 5 per cent on gross sales.

IV. Retail dealers in liquor, including distilled spirits, fermented liquors and wines of every description, shall pay one hundred dollars and ten per centum on the gross amount of all sales made.

Retail dealers in liquors, $100 and 10 per cent. on gross sales.

V. Retail dealers whose quarterly sales shall exceed one hundred dollars, and shall be less than five hundred dollars, shall pay twenty-five dollars, and two and a-half per centum on the gross amount of sales made; and where quarterly sales exceed five hundred dollars, the specific tax shall be fifty dollars, and two-and-a-half per centum on the gross amount of sales made. Every person whose business or occupation it is to sell or offer to sell groceries or any goods, wares, merchandise or other things of foreign or domestic production, in less quantities than a whole original piece or package at one time, to the same person, (not including wines, spirituous or malt liquors,) shall be regarded as a retail dealer under this act: *Provided, however*, That any mechanic, who shall sell only the products of the labor of himself and his own family, shall be exempt from this tax.

Retail dealers when quarterly sales over $100 and less than $500, less than $25 and when over $500, $50 specific tax and 2½ per cent. on sales.

VI. Wholesale dealers shall pay two hundred dollars and two and a half per centum on the gross amount of all sales made. Every person whose business or occupation it is to sell or offer to sell groceries, or any goods, wares or merchandise, of foreign or domestic production, by one or more original packages or pieces at one time to the same purchaser, not including wines, spirituous or malt liquors, and every person whose business it is to sell or offer to sell slaves, shall be deemed as a wholesale dealer under this act; but having been registered as a wholesale dealer, such person may also sell, as aforesaid, as a retailer. *Provided*, That contractors working for, and selling their own products exclusively to the Confederate States, to an amount not exceeding five thousand dollars a year, and such dealers as sell exclusively to consumers, and not to others to sell again, shall not be regarded as wholesale, but as retail dealers.

Wholesale dealers $200 and two and a half per cent.

VII. Pawnbrokers shall pay two hundred dollars. Every person, whose business or occupation it is to take or receive, by way of pledge, favor or exchange, any goods, wares or merchandize, or any kind of personal property whatever, for the repayment or security of money lent thereon, shall be deemed a pawnbroker under this act.

Pawnbrokers, $200.

VIII. Distillers shall pay two hundred dollars, and twenty per centum on the gross amount of all sales made; and also, twenty per centum on the value of all liquors distilled for any other person, and the tax on distillers shall be a lien on the still or stills used, and upon the other fixtures and articles for carrying on the business, and shall have priority over all other liens or claims. Every person or co-partnership, who distills or manufactures spirituous liquors for sale, shall be deemed a distiller under this act: *Provided however*, That distillers of fruit, for ninety days or less, shall pay sixty dollars, and also fifty cents per gallon on the first ten gallons, and two dollars per gallon on all spirits distilled beyond that quantity.

Distillers $200, 20 per cent. on sales, and same on value of liquors distilled for others.

Of fruit for 90 days $60.

IX. Brewers shall pay one hundred dollars, and two and a half per centum on the gross amount of sales made. Every person, who manufactures fermented liquors of any name or description for sale from malt, wholly or in part, shall be deemed a brewer under this act.

Brewers, $100 and 2½ per cent.

X. Hotels, inns, taverns and eating houses shall be classified and rated according to the yearly rental, or if not rented, according to the estimated value of the yearly rental of the house or property occupied or intended to be occupied as a hotel, inn, tavern or eating house, as follows, to-wit: in cases where the actual or estimated rent shall amount to ten thousand dollars, or more, they shall constitute the first class, and pay an annual sum of five hundred dollars; in cases where said rent shall be five thousand dollars and less than ten thousand dollars, they shall constitute the second class, and pay an annual sum of three hundred dollars; and in cases where said rent shall be two thousand and five hundred dollars, and less than five thousand dollars, they shall constitute the third class, and pay

Hotels, inns, &c.

1st class, $500.

2d class, $300

3d class, $200. an annual sum of two hundred dollars; in cases where said rent shall be one thousand dollars, and less than two thousand five hundred dollars, they shall constitute the fourth class, and pay

4th class, $100. an annual sum of one hundred dollars; and in cases where said rent shall be less than one thousand dollars, they shall constitute the fifth

5th class, $30. class, and pay an annual sum of thirty dollars. Every place where food and lodgings, or lodgings only, are provided for and furnished travellers, sojourners or boarders in view of payment therefor, the income or receipts from which amount to five hundred dollars from that source, shall be regarded a hotel, inn or tavern under this act.

XI. That every place where food or refreshments of any kind are provided for casual visitors and sold for consumption therein, and every boarding house in which there shall be six boarders, or more, shall be deemed an eating house under this act.

Brokers, $200. XII. Brokers shall pay two hundred dollars. Any person whose business it is to purchase and sell stocks, coined money, bank notes or other securities, for themselves or others, or who deals in exchanges relating to money, shall be deemed a broker under this act.

Commercial brokers, $200 and 2½ per cent. XIII. Commercial brokers or commission merchants shall pay two hundred dollars, and two and a half per centum upon all sales made. Any person or firm, except one registered as a wholesale dealer or banker, whose business it is, as the agent of others, to purchase or sell goods, or seek orders therefor in original or unbroken packages, or produce consigned by others than the producers, to manage business matters for the owners of vessels, or for the shippers or consignors of goods, or whose business it is to purchase, rent, hire or sell real estate or negroes, shall be deemed a commercial broker or commission merchant under this act.

Tobacconists $50 and 2½ per cent. XIV. Tobacconists shall pay fifty dollars and two and a half per cent. on gross amount of sales. Any person whose business it is to sell, at retail, cigars, snuff, or tobacco in any form, shall be deemed a tobacconist under this act. But registered wholesale and retail dealers shall not be taxed as tobacconists.

Theatres, $500 and 5 per cent. on receipts. XV. Theatres shall pay five hundred dollars, and five per cent. on all receipts, which tax shall be paid by the owner of the building. Every edifice used for the purpose of dramatic representations, plays or performances, and not including halls rented or used occasionally for concerts or theatrical representations, shall be regarded as a theatre

Circus, $100. $10 each exhibition. under this act. Each circus shall pay one hundred dollars, and a tax of ten dollars for each exhibition, which tax shall be paid by the manager thereof. Every building, tent or space, or area, where feats of horsemanship or arobatic sports are exhibited, shall be regarded as

Jugglers, $50. a circus under this act. Jugglers and other persons exhibiting shows, shall pay fifty dollars. Every person who performs by slight of hand shall be regarded as a juggler under this act: *Provided*, That no registry made in one State shall be held to authorize exhibitions in another State; and but one registry shall be required under this act to authorize exhibitions in any one State.

Bowling alleys and billiard rooms $40. XVI. Bowling alleys and billiard rooms shall pay forty dollars for each alley or billiard table registered, which tax shall be paid by the owner thereof. Every place or building where bowls are thrown or billiards played, and open to the public, with or without price, shall be regarded as a bowling alley or billiard room respectively under this act.

XVII. Livery stable keepers shall pay fifty dollars. Any person whose occupation or business is to keep horses for hire or to let, shall be regarded as a livery stable keeper under this act. Livery stables, $50.

XVIII. Cattle brokers shall pay the sum of fifty dollars, and two and half per centum on the gross amount of sales made. Any person whose business it is to buy and sell and deal in cattle, horses, hogs or sheep, shall be considered a cattle broker. Cattle brokers, $50, and 2½ per cent.

XIX. Butchers and bakers shall pay the sum of fifty dollars, and one per centum on the gross amount of sales made. Any person whose business it is to butcher and sell, or offer for sale in open market or otherwise, the flesh of cattle, hogs or sheep, shall be deemed a butcher under this act; and any person whose business it is to bake and sell, or offer for sale, bread, shall be deemed a baker under this act. Butchers and bakers, $50 and 1 per cent.

XX. Pedlers shall pay fifty dollars, and two and a half per centum on the gross sales. Any person, except persons engaged in peddling exclusively periodicals, books, newspapers, published in the Confederate States, bibles, or religious tracts, who sells, or offers to sell, at retail, goods, wares, or other commodities, travelling with his goods from place to place in the street, or through different parts of the country, shall be deemed a pedler under this act: *Provided*, That any pedler who sells, or offers to sell, dry goods, foreign or domestic, by one or more original pieces or packages at one time, and to the same person or person's as aforesaid, shall pay one hundred dollars, and two and a half per cent. on the gross sales; and any person who peddles jewelry shall pay fifty dollars, and two and a half per centum on the gross sales. The tax upon pedlers shall be deemed a tax upon the personal privilege, to be paid by each individual engaged in the business, without regard to place at which the same is conducted. Pedlers, $50 and 2½ per cent. Books, newspapers, &c., exempt. Selling by the package, $100 and 2½ per cent. Jewelry, $50 and 2½ per cent.

XXI. Apothecaries shall pay fifty dollars, and two and a half per centum on the gross amount of sales made. Every person who keeps a shop or building where medicines are compounded or prepared according to prescriptions of physicians, and sold, shall be regarded as an apothecary under this act. Apothecaries $50 and 2½ per cent.

XXII. Photographers shall pay the sum of fifty dollars, and two and a half per centum on the gross amount of sales made. Any person or persons who make for sale photographs, ambrotypes, daguerreotypes, or pictures on glass, metal, paper or other material, by the action of light, shall be regarded a photographer under this act. Photographers, $50 and 2½ per cent.

XXIII. Lawyers actually engaged in practice shall pay fifty dollars. Every person whose business it is for fee or reward, to prosecute or defend causes in any court of record or other judicial tribunal of the Confederate States, or of any State, or give advice in relation to causes or matters pending therein, shall be deemed to be a lawyer within the meaning of this act. Lawyers, $50.

XXIV. Physicians, surgeons and dentists actually engaged in the practice shall pay fifty dollars. Every person whose business it is, for fee or reward, to prescribe remedies, or perform surgical operations for the cure of any bodily disease or ailing, shall be deemed a physician, surgeon or dentist within the meaning of this act, as the case may be; and the provisions of paragraph number twenty-one shall not Physicians, surgeons and dentists, $50.

extend to physicians who keep on hand medicines solely for the purpose of making up their own prescriptions for their own patients. The tax upon lawyers, physicians, surgeons and dentists shall be deemed a tax upon the personal privilege, to be paid by each individual in the business, and without regard to the place at which the same is conducted: *Provided*, That the provisions of this act shall not apply to physicians and surgeons exclusively engaged in the Confederate service.

Surgeons and physicians in the army exempt.

Confectioners, $50 and 2½ per cent.

XXV. Confectioners shall pay fifty dollars and two and a half per centum on the gross amount of sales. Every person who sells at retail confectionery, sweetmeats, comfits, or other confects, in any building, shall be regarded as a confectioner under this act.

LIST AND RETURN OF REGISTERED BUSINESS.

Registered persons to make return 1st July, 1861.

SEC. 5. And every person registered and taxed upon the gross amount of sales as aforesaid shall be required, on the first day of July, eighteen hundred and sixty-three, to make a list or return to the assessor of the district of the gross amount of such sales as aforesaid, to-wit: From the passage of this act to the thirtieth day of June, eighteen hundred and sixty-three, inclusive, and at the end of every three months, or within twenty days thereafter, after the said first day of July, eighteen hundred and sixty three, make a list or return to the assessor of the district, of the gross amount of such sales made as aforesaid, with the amount of tax which has accrued, or should accrue thereon, which list shall have annexed thereto a declaration, under oath or affirmation, in form or manner as may be prescribed by the commissioner of taxes, that the same is true and correct, and shall, within such time as the collector may designate, by public notice, which time shall not be less than ten nor more than thirty days from the date of such notice, pay to the collector the amount of tax thereupon, as aforesaid, and in default thereof, shall pay a penalty in double the amount of the tax.

To be returned under oath.

SALARIES.

Salaries—1 per c't. on first $1,500, 2 per cent. on excess over $1,500. Military and naval exempt.

SEC. 6. That upon the salaries of all salaried persons serving in any capacity whatever, except upon the salaries of persons in the military or naval service, there shall be levied and collected a tax of one per centum on the gross amount of such salary, when not exceeding fifteen hundred dollars, and two per centum upon an excess over that amount, to be levied and collected at the end of each year, in the manner prescribed for other taxes enumerated in this act: *Provided*, That no taxes shall be imposed by virtue of this act on the salary of any person receiving a salary not exceeding one thousand dollars per annum, or at a like rate for another period of time, longer or shorter.

Salaries less than $1,000 exempt.

INCOMES FROM ALL VOCATIONS.

Incomes and profits assessed first January.

SEC. 7. That the Secretary of the Treasury shall cause to be assessed and ascertained, on the first day of January next, or as soon thereafter as practicable, the income and profits derived by each person, joint stock company and corporation from every occupation, employment or business, whether registered or not, in which they may have been engaged, and from every investment of labor, skill, property or money, and the income and profits derived from any source whatever, except salaries, during the calendar year preceding the said first day of January next, and the said income and profits shall be ascertained, assessed and taxed in the manner hereinafter prescribed. Except salaries.

RENTS.

I. If the income be derived from the rents of houses, lands, tenements, manufacturing or mining establishments, fixtures and machinery, mills, springs of salt or oil, or veins of coal, iron or other minerals, there shall be deducted from the gross amount of the annual rent a sum sufficient for the necessary annual repairs, not exceeding ten per centum on said rent, except that the rent derived from houses shall be subject to a deduction not exceeding five per centum for annual repairs. Rents from houses, lands, &c. 10 per cent. deducted, 5 per ct. from rent of houses.

MANUFACTURING, ETC.

II. If the income be derived from any manufacturing or mining business, there shall be deducted from the gross value of the products of the year; first, the rent of the establishment and fixtures, if actually rented, and not owned by the person prosecuting the business; second, the cost of the labor actually hired and paid for; third, the actual cost of the raw material purchased and manufactured; fourth, if the income be derived from the production of pig metal or bloom iron, from the ore, there shall be deducted the cost of labor, food, and necessary repairs. Manufacturing and mining.

NAVIGATING ENTERPRISES.

III. If the income be derived from navigating enterprises, there shall be deducted from the gross earnings, including the value of freights on goods shipped by the person running the vessel, the hire of the boat or vessel, if not owned by the person running the same, or if owned by him, a reasonable allowance for the wear and tear of the same, not exceeding ten per cent. per annum, and also the cost of running the boat or vessel. Navigating. 10 per cent. deducted.

SHIP BUILDING, ETC.

IV. If the income be derived by the tax payer from boat or ship-building, there shall be deducted from the gross receipts of his occupation, including the value of the ship when finished, if built for himself, the cost of the labor actually hired and paid by himself, and the prime cost of the materials, if purchased by him. Ship and boat building.

SALES OF MERCHANDIZE AND OTHER PROPERTY.

V. If the income be derived by the tax payer from the sale of merchandize or any other property, real or personal, there shall be deducted from the gross amount of sales, the prime cost of the property sold, including the cost of transportation, salaries of clerks actually paid, and the rent of the buildings employed in the business, if hired and not owned by himself. Sale of merchandize.

ALL OTHER OCCUPATIONS.

From any other business, salaries of clerks and rent of office, &c., deducted.

VI. If the income be derived by the tax payer from any other occupation, profession, employment or business, there shall be deducted from the gross amount of fees, compensation, profits, earnings, or commissions, the salaries of clerks actually paid, and the rent of the office or other building used in the business, if hired and not owned by himself, the cost of labor actually paid and not owned by himself, and the cost of material other than machinery purchased for the use of his business, or to be converted into some other form in the course of his business; and in case of mutual insurance companies, the amount of losses paid by them during the year. The income derived from all other sources shall be subject to no deduction whatever; nor shall foreigners be subject to a tax upon any other income than that derived from property owned, or occupations or employments pursued by them within the Confederate States, and in estimating income there shall be included the value of the estimated annual rental of all dwellings, houses, buildings or building lots in cities, towns, or villages, occupied by the owners, or owned and not occupied or hired, and the value of the estimated annual hire of all slaves not engaged on plantations or farms, and not employed in some business or occupations, the profits of which are taxed as income under this act. When the income shall be thus ascertained, all of those which do not exceed five hundred dollars per annum shall be exempt from taxation. On all incomes received during the year over five hundred dollars and not exceeding fifteen hundred dollars, a tax of five per cent. shall be paid; on all incomes over fifteen hundred dollars, and less than three thousand dollars, five per cent. shall be paid on the first fifteen hundred dollars, and ten per cent. on all excess; on all incomes of (or) over three thousand dollars, and less than five thousand dollars, a tax of ten per cent. shall be paid; on all incomes of (or) over five thousand dollars and less than ten thousand dollars, a tax of twelve and a half per cent. shall be paid; and on all incomes of (or) over ten thousand dollars, a tax of fifteen per cent. shall be paid. All joint stock companies and corporations shall reserve one-tenth of the annual earnings, set apart for dividend and reserved fund, to be paid to the collector of the Confederate tax, and the dividend then paid to the stockholder shall not be estimated as a part of his income for the purposes of this act. All persons shall give in an estimate of their income and profits derived from any other source whatever, and in doing so shall first state the gross amount of their receipts as individuals or members of a firm or partnership, and, also, state particularly each item for which a deduction is to be made and the amount to be deducted for it: *Provided*, That the incomes and profits upon which the above tax is to be imposed shall not be deemed to include the products of land which are taxed in kind, as hereinafter described: *Provided further*, That in case the annual earnings of said joint stock companies and corporations set apart as aforesaid, shall give a profit of more than ten and less than twenty per cent. upon their capital stock paid in, one-eighth of said sum so set apart shall be paid as a tax to the collector aforesaid, and in case said sum so set apart shall give a profit of more than twenty per cent. on their capital stock paid in, one-sixth thereof shall be reserved and paid as aforesaid. The tax levied in this section shall

Incomes from all other sources subject to no deduction.

Foreigners doing business in Confederate States.

Incomes not exceeding $500 exempt.

Incomes over $500 and not exceeding $1,500, 5 per cent.; over $1,500 and less than $3,000, five per cent. upon 1st $1,500 and 10 per cent on excess; over $3,000 and less than $5000, 10 per cent., over $5000 and less than $10000, 12½ per cent.; all over $10,000 15 per ct.

Corporations, &c to reserve one-tenth annual earnings.

Not to include products of land taxed in kind.

be paid on the first day of January next, and on the first day of January of each year thereafter. Amended June 14. Sec. 4 p. II

Tax to be collected 1st day of January.

FALSE RETURNS. REFEREES.

SEC. 8. That if the assessor shall be dissatisfied with the statement or estimate of income and profits derived from any source whatever, other than products in kind, which the tax payer is required to render, or with any deduction claimed by said tax payer, he shall select one disinterested citizen of the vicinage, as a referee, and the tax payer shall select another, and the two thus selected shall call in a third, who shall investigate and determine the facts in reference to said estimate and deductions, and fix the amount of income and profits on which the tax payer shall be assessed, and a certificate signed by a majority of the referees, shall be conclusive as to the amount of income and profits on which the tax payer shall be assessed: *Provided*, That if any person shall fail or refuse to render the statement or estimate aforesaid, or shall fail or refuse to select a referee as aforesaid, the assessor shall select three referees, who shall fix the amount of income and profits on which the tax payer shall be assessed from the best evidence they can obtain, and a certificate signed by a majority of said referees shall be conclusive on the tax payer: *And provided further*, That in any case submitted to referees, if they, or a majority of them, shall find and certify that the statement or estimate of income and profits rendered by the tax payer does not contain more than four-fifths of the true and real amount of his taxable income and profits, then the tax payer, in addition to the income tax on the true amount of his income and profits ascertained and assessed by the referees, shall pay ten per centum on the amount of said income tax, and the assessor shall be entitled to one-fifth of said additional ten per centum over and above all other fees and allowances: *And provided further*, That the assessor may administer oaths to referees, the tax payer, and any witness before the referees, in regard to said estimate, and any deduction claimed, or any fact in reference thereto, in such form as the Secretary of the Treasury may prescribe.

Referees to be selected when assessor is not satisfied with return.

Certificate of referees conclusive against tax payer.

If statement contains less than four fifths of true am't. tax payer to pay 10 per cent. on amount.

Assessor entitled to one-fifth of the 10 per cent.

Assessor may administer oaths.

PROFITS ON FLOUR, BACON, ETC., DURING THE YEAR 1862.

SEC. 9. On all profits made by any person, partnership, or corporation during the year eighteen hundred and sixty-two, by the purchase within the Confederate States and sale, during the said year, of any flour, corn, bacon, pork, oats, hay, rice, salt, or iron, or the manufactures of iron, sugar, molasses made of cane, leather, woolen cloths, shoes, boots, blankets and cotton cloths, a tax of ten per centum shall be levied and collected, to be paid on the first day of July next: *Provided*, That the tax imposed by this section shall not apply to purchases and sales made in the due course of the regular retail business, and shall not continue beyond the present year.

Profits on flour, bacon, pork, &c., during the year 1862, 10 per cent. to be paid 1st July, 1863.

TAX IN KIND.

SEC. 10. That each farmer and planter in the Confederate States, ~~after reserving for his own use fifty bushels of sweet potatoes, and fifty bushels of Irish potatoes, one hundred bushels of the corn, or fifty bushels of the wheat produced in the present year~~, shall pay and deliver to the Confederate Government, of the products of the present year, one-tenth of the wheat, corn, oats, rye, buckwheat or rice, ~~sweet~~

~~50 bushels sweet potatoes, 50 bushels Irish potatoes, 100 bushels corn, 50 bushels wheat reserved.~~

One-tenth of the wheat, corn, &c., as a tax in kind.

and Irish potatoes, and of the cured hay and fodder; also one tenth of the sugar, molasses made of cane or of sorghum, where more than thirty gallons are made, cotton, wool and tobacco; the cotton ginned and packed in some secure manner, and tobacco stripped and packed in boxes; the cotton to be delivered by him on or before the first day of March, and the tobacco on or before the first day of July, next after their production. Each farmer or planter, after reserving twenty bushels of peas or beans, but not more than twenty bushels of both, for his own use, shall deliver to the Confederate Government, for its use, one-tenth of the peas, beans and ground peas produced and gathered by him during the present year. As soon as each of the aforesaid crops are made ready for market, the tax assessor, in case of disagreement between him and the tax payer, shall proceed to estimate the same in the following manner: The assessor and tax payer shall each select a disinterested freeholder from the vicinage, who may call in a third in case of difference of opinion, to settle the matter in dispute; or if the tax payer neglects or refuses to select one such freeholder, the said assessor shall select two, who shall proceed to assess the crops as herein provided. They shall ascertain the amount of the crops either by actual measurement or by computing the contents of the rooms or houses in which they are held, when a correct computation is practicable by such a method, and the appraisers shall then estimate under oath, the quantity and quality of said crops, including what may have been sold or consumed by the producer prior to said estimates, whether gathered or not; excepting from said estimates such portion of said crops as may be necessary to raise and fatten the hogs of such farmer, planter or grazier, for pork; *Provided*, That the following persons shall be exempt from the payment of the tax in kind, imposed by this section, viz:

Reserve 20 bushels peas or beans, or 20 bushels of both.

Referees to be selected.

May call in a third person.

Appraisers to estimate, under oath, the quantity, quality and value of the produce.

Exemptions, each family not worth more than $500.

I. Each head of a family not worth more [than] five hundred dollars.

$500, and for each minor $100, $500 for each minor living, lost, or disabled in the army.

II. Each head of a family with minor children, not worth more than five hundred dollars for himself, and one hundred dollars for each minor living with him, and five hundred dollars in addition thereto, for each minor son he has living, or may have lost, or had disabled in the military or naval service.

$100 each officer &c., in the army &c., or discharged for wounds.

III. Each officer, soldier or seaman, in the army or navy, or who has been discharged therefrom for wounds, and is not worth more than one thousand dollars.

IV. Each widow of any officer, soldier or seaman, who has died in the military or naval service, the widow not worth more than one thousand dollars: *Provided*, That in all cases where the farmer or planter does not produce more than fifty bushels of Irish potatoes, two hundred bushels of corn, or twenty bushels of peas and beans, he shall not be subject to the tax in kind on said articles, or either of them; and the forage derived from the corn plant, shall also be exempt in all cases where the corn is not taxed in kind; neither shall any farmer or planter, who does not produce more than ten pounds of wool or more fifteen pounds of ginned cotton, for each member of the family, be subject to said tax in kind. The tax assessor, after allowing the exemptions authorized in this section, shall assess the value of the portion of said crops to which the Government is entitled, and shall give a written statement of this estimate to the collector, and a copy of the same to the producer. The said producer shall be required

50 bushels Irish potatoes, 200 bushels corn, 20 bushels peas and beans exempt.

10lbs. wool, 15 lbs. cotton for each member of family, exempt.

to deliver the wheat, corn, oats, rye, buckwheat, rice, peas, beans, cured hay and fodder, sugar, molasses of cane or sorghum, wool, thus to be paid as a tithe in kind, after they have been estimated as aforesaid, in such form and ordinary marketable condition as may be usual in the section in which they are to be delivered, within thirty days from the date of notice given by the agent of collection, that he is ready to receive such produce, (except cotton and tobacco shall be delivered in the manner, and at the times hereinbefore provided,) at some depot not more than twelve miles from the place of production, and if not delivered by the times, and in the order stated, he shall be liable to pay five times the estimated value of the portion aforesaid, to be collected by the tax collector, as hereinafter prescribed: *Provided*, That Post Quartermasters may direct such delivery to be made at any time within [illegible] months after the date of said estimates, under the sanction of the penalty aforesaid, and that producers shall be paid the expenses of the transportation of their tithes from the place of production to the place of delivery at the usual rates of compensation paid by the Government in the State in which the delivery is made. Such delivery when required to be made of grain in bushels, shall be made in bushels, according to the Government standard of weight per bushel: *Provided*, The government shall be bound to furnish to the producer sacks for the delivery of such articles of grain as require to be put in sacks for transportation, and shall allow to the producer of molasses the cost of the barrels containing the same. The said estimate shall be conclusive evidence of the amount in money, of tax due by the producer to the government, and the collector is hereby authorized to proceed to collect the same by issuing a warrant of distress from his office, under his signature, in the nature of a writ of *fieri facias*, and by virtue of the same to seize and sell any personal property on the premises of the tax payer or elsewhere, belonging to him, or so much thereof as may be necessary for the purpose of paying the tax, and the increase aforesaid and costs; and said sale shall be made in the manner and form and after the notice required by the laws of the several States for judicial sales of personal property, and the said warrant of distress may be executed by the tax collector or any deputy by him appointed for that purpose, and the deputy, executing the warrant shall be entitled to the same fees as are allowed in the respective States to sheriffs executing writs of *fieri facias*, said fees to be paid as costs by the tax payer: *Provided*, That in all cases where the assessor and tax payer agree on the assessment of the crops, and the value of the portion thereof to which the government is entitled, no other assessment shall be necessary; but the estimate agreed on shall be reduced to writing and signed by the assessor and tax payer, and have the same force and effect as the assessment and estimate of disinterested freeholders hereinbefore mentioned; and two copies of such assessment and estimate thus agreed on and signed as aforesaid shall be made, and one delivered to the producer and the other to the collector; *And provided further*, That the assessor is hereby authorized to administer oaths to the tax payers and to witnesses in regard to any item of the estimate herein required to be made: *And provided further*, When agricultural produce in kind is paid for taxes, if payment be made by a tenant who is bound to pay his rent in kind, the tenth part of said rent in kind shall be paid in kind by the tenant

[illegible] June 10. 64

Sacks to be furnished by the government and cost of barrels to be allowed.

Estimate conclusive of amount of tax in money.

Collector to issue warrant of distress in case of default.

Notice for sales of distrained property.

Fees allowed.

Assessor and tax payer may agree upon assessment of crops and value of the tithes.

Assessor to administer oaths.

Tenant pay the lessor of rent and lessor to be released from including same in his statement.

to the government as and for the tax of the lessor on said rent, and the receipt of the government officer shall release the lessor from all obligation to include such rent in kind in his statement of income, and discharge the tenant from so much of his rent to the lessor.

SLAUGHTERED HOGS, ETC.

Account of slaughtered hogs to be exhibited to assessor on first March.

amended June 10. 1864.

One-tenth same to be delivered as an equivalent, at rate of 60 pounds bacon to 100 lbs. pork.

1st Nov. estimate of cattle, mules, &c., to be made, one per cent. on value, to be paid 1st Jan.

Gross sales of beeves prior to 1st Nov. taxed as income, deducting purchase money & value of corn consumed.

In case of disagreement, referees to be selected.

SEC. 11. That every farmer, planter, or grazier, or other person who slaughters hogs, shall exhibit to the assessor, on or about the first of March, eighteen hundred and sixty ~~four~~ an account of all the hogs he may have slaughtered since the passage of this act and before that time; after the delivery of this estimate to the post quartermaster hereinafter mentioned by the assessor, the said farmer, planter or grazier shall deliver an equivalent for one-tenth of the same in cured bacon, at the rate of sixty pounds of bacon to the one hundred weight of pork. That on the first of November, eighteen hundred and sixty three, an estimate shall be made, as hereinbefore provided, of the value of all neat cattle, horses, mules, not used in cultivation, and asses owned by each person in the Confederate States, and upon such value the said owners shall be taxed one per cent., to be paid on or before the first day of January next ensuing. If the grazier, or planter or farmer shall have sold beeves since the passage of this act, and prior to the first day of November, the gross proceeds of such sales shall be estimated and taxed as income, after deducting therefrom the money actually paid for the purchase of such beeves, if they have been actually purchased, and the value of the corn or peas consumed by them. The estimate of these items shall be made in case of disagreement between the assessor and tax payer as herein provided in other cases of income tax: *Provided*, That no farmer, planter or grazier, or other person, who shall not slaughter more than two hundred and fifty pounds of net pork during any year, shall be subject to the bacon tithe imposed by this section; and every officer, soldier, or seaman, in the military or naval service, or who may have been discharged therefrom on account of wounds, or physical disability, and any widow of such officer, soldier or seaman, or any head of a family, who does not own more than two cows and calves, shall be exempt from the tax imposed by this section on neat cattle.

POST QUARTERMASTERS.

Post quartermasters. One for collection of articles, the other for distribution of them.

Assessor to transfer estimates to post quartermaster, taking his receipt.

Copy of receipt to be furnished the auditor by chief collector.

SEC. 12. That the Secretary of War shall divide the service of the quartermaster's department into two branches, one, herein denominated post quartermasters, for the collection of the articles paid for taxes in kind, and the other for distribution to the proper points for supplying the army, and for delivering cotton and tobacco to the agents of the Secretary of the Treasury. The tax assessor shall transfer the estimate of articles due from each person, by way of a tax in kind, to the duly authorized post quartermaster, taking from the said quartermaster a receipt which shall be filed as a voucher with the chief collector in settling his account, and a copy of this receipt shall be furnished by the chief collector to the auditor settling the post quartermaster's account as a charge against him. The post quartermaster receiving the estimate, shall collect from the tax payer the articles which it specifies, and which he is bound to pay and deliver as a tax to the Confederate government. The post quartermaster shall be liable for the safe custody of the articles placed in his care, and shall account for the same by showing that, after proper deductions from unavoidable loss, the residue has been delivered to the distributing agents as evidenced by their receipts. The said post quartermaster shall, also, state the accounts of the quartermaster's receiving from him the articles delivered in payment of taxes in kind at his depot, and make a monthly report of the same to such officer as the Secretary of War may designate: *Provided*, That in case the post quartermaster shall be unable to collect the tax in kind specified in the estimate delivered to him as aforesaid, he shall deliver to the district tax collector said estimate as a basis for the distress warrant authorized to be issued, and take a receipt therefor, and forward the same to the chief tax collector as a credit in the statement of the accounts of said post quartermaster: *Provided*, That any partial payment of said tax in kind shall be endorsed on said estimate before delivering the same to the district tax collector as aforesaid, and the receipt given to him therefor by the district tax collector, shall specify said partial payment. When the articles thus collected through the payment of taxes in kind have been received at the depot as aforesaid, they shall be distributed to the agents of the Secretary of the Treasury, if they consist of cotton, wool or tobacco, or if they be suitable for forage or subsistence, to such places and in such manner as the Secretary of War may prescribe. The wool collected under this act shall be retained by the Quartermaster's Department as supplies. Should the Secretary of War find that some of the agricultural produce thus paid in and suitable for forage and subsistence has been, or will be deposited in places where it cannot be used either directly or indirectly for these purposes, he shall cause the same to be sold, in such manner as he may prescribe, and the proceeds of such sale shall be paid into the Treasury of the Confederate States. Should, however, the Secretary of War notify the Secretary of the Treasury that it would be impracticable for him to collect or use the articles taxed in kind, or any of them, to be received in certain districts or localities, then the Secretary of the Treasury shall proceed to collect in said district or locality the money value of said articles specified in said estimate and not required in kind, and said money value shall be due on the first day of January in each and every year, and be collected as soon thereafter as practicable, and where in districts heretofore or which may hereafter be ascertained to be so impracticable, quartermasters or commissaries serving with troops in the field, shall have collected or may hereafter collect from producers any portion of their tax in kind, the receipts of such officers shall be held good to the producers against the collection of the money value of their tax, to the extent and value of such portions as may have been or may be hereafter collected. And when assessments in practicable localities have been made and transferred to post quartermasters, and transportation is difficult to be obtained, the supply of grain sacks insufficient, or the amount of produce receivable is too small to justify the expenses of collection, post quartermasters, with approval of their superior officers, shall be authorized to transfer the estimates to District Collectors, to be collected in their money value only.

Post quartermaster to collect articles & be responsible for their safe custody.

Post quartermaster to state the accounts of the quartermaster's receiving the articles delivered.

If post quartermasters fail to collect articles estimated to be delivered to district collector.

Partial payment of tax in kind to be endorsed on estimate.

Cotton, wool, & tobacco distributed to agents of Secretary of the Treasury.

Forage, &c., under control of Secretary of War.

If in places where it cannot be used, shall cause same to be sold and proceeds paid in to treasury.

In certain districts money value of articles may be collected.

Money value to be due 1st January every year.

SEC. 13. That the assessors, whose duty it is under said act to estimate the taxes in kind, shall be appointed by the Secretary of War, and their duties shall be the same, and the duties shall be executed in the same manner as is prescribed by sections ten, eleven and twelve of this act, in reference to the estimates and assessment of taxes in kind on agricultural products and slaughtered hogs; and there may be one assessor appointed for each practicable tax district, and he shall take the oath as assessor of taxes in kind prescribed by section five of the act for the assessment and collection of taxes, approved May first, eighteen hundred and sixty-three, which oath shall be delivered to such officer as the Secretary of War may designate. And the assessors of taxes in kind shall be separate and distinct from the assessors of money tax, and shall be subject to the exclusive direction and control of the War Department, and shall receive the same compensation for such time as they may be employed, as is allowed to other agents of the Quartermaster's Department.

ESTIMATES OF INCOMES AND STATEMENTS OF SPECIFIC TAX, ETC.

Estimates of incomes, &c., delivered by assessor to collector, and give receipt.

SEC. 14. That the estimates of incomes and profits, other than those payable in kind, and the statements or bills for the amount of the specific tax on occupations, employments, business and professions, and of taxes on gross sales, shall be delivered by the assessor to the collector of the district, who shall give him a receipt for the same, and the said assessor shall file his receipt with the chief tax collector of the State, and the collector of the district, holding said estimates, statements or bills, shall proceed to collect the same from the tax payer. The money thus collected shall be paid to the chief tax collector of the State, and the estimates, statements or bills aforesaid, shall be arranged by the assessor, and general lists shall be made from them in the same manner and for the same purposes designated by section thirteen of the assessment act.

Receipt to be filed with chief collector by the assessor.

Money to be paid to chief collector accompanied by estimates, &c.

TRUSTEES, GUARDIANS, EXECUTORS, ETC.

Fiduciaries answerable for all taxables in their care and requirde to pay the taxes, &c.

SEC. 15. That every person who, as trustee, guardian, tutor, curator or committee, executor or administrator, or as agent, attorney in fact, or factor, of any person or persons, whether residing in the Confederate States or not, and every receiver in chancery, clerk, register or other officer of any court, shall be answerable for the doing of all such acts, matters and things as shall be required to be done in order to the assessment of the money, property, products and income under their control, and the payment of taxes thereon, and shall be indemnified against all and every person for all payments on account of the taxes herein specified, and shall be responsible for all taxes due from the estates, income money, or property in their possession or under their control.

Indemnified for payment of such taxes.

INCOMES EXEMPT.

Incomes of hospitals, asylums, churches, schools and colleges exempt.

SEC. 16. The income and moneys of hospitals, asylums, churches, schools and colleges shall be exempt from taxation under the provisions of this act.

RULES AND REGULATIONS.

SEC. 17. That the Secretary of the Treasury be, and he is hereby authorized to make all rules and regulations necessary to the operation of this act, and not inconsistent herewith. Secretary of Treasury rules, &c

LIFE OF THE ACT.

SEC. 18. This act shall be in force for two years after the expiration of the present year, and the taxes herein imposed for the present year, shall be levied and collected each year thereafter in the manner and form herein prescribed, and for the said time of two years, unless this act shall be sooner repealed. Act in force two years after expiration of 1863.

Approved February 17, 1864.

THE TAX BILL.

AN ACT, to lay additional taxes for the common defence and support of the Government.

February 17. 1864

SEC. 1. *The Congress of the Confederate States of America do enact,* That in addition to the taxes levied by the "Act to lay taxes for the common defence and to carry on the Government of the Confederate States," approved twenty-fourth of April, eighteen hundred and sixty-three, there shall be levied, from the passage of this act, on the subjects of taxation hereafter mentioned, and collected from every person, co-partnership, association or corporation, liable therefor, taxes as follows, to-wit:

I. Upon the value of property, real, personal and mixed, of every kind and description, not hereinafter excepted or taxed at a different rate, five per cent: *Provided,* That from this tax on the value of property, employed in agriculture, shall be deducted the value of the tax in kind derived therefrom, as assessed under the law imposing it, and delivered to the Government: *Provided,* That no credit shall be allowed beyond five per cent.

II. On the value of gold and silver wares and plate, jewels, jewelry and watches, ten per cent.

III. The value of property taxed under this section, shall be assessed on the basis of the market value of the same, or similar property in the neighborhood where assessed in the year eighteen hundred and sixty, except in cases where land, slaves, cotton or tobacco have been purchased since the first day of January, eighteen hundred and sixty-two, in which case the said land, slaves, cotton and tobacco so purchased, shall be assessed at the price actually paid for the same by the owner.

SEC. 2. On the value of all shares or interests held in any bank, banking company or association, canal, navigation, importing and exporting, insurance, manufacturing, telegraph, express, railroad, and dry dock companies, and all other joint stock companies of every kind, whether incorporated or not, five per cent.

The value of property taxed under this section shall be assessed upon the basis of the market value of said property in the neighborhood where assessed, in such currency as may be in general use there, in the purchase and sale of such property, at the time of assessment.

SEC. 3. I. Upon the amount of all gold and silver coin, gold dust, gold or silver bullion, whether held by the banks or other corporations or individuals, five per cent; and upon all monies held abroad, or upon the amount of all bills of exchange, drawn therefor on foreign countries, a tax of five per cent; such tax upon money abroad to be assessed and collected according to the value thereof at the place where the tax is paid.

II. Upon the amount of all solvent credits, and of all bank bills, and all other papers issued as currency, exclusive of non-interest bearing Confederate treasury notes, and not employed in a registered business, the income derived from which is taxed, five per cent.

Sec. 4. Upon profits made in trade and business, as follows:

I. On all profits made by buying and selling spirituous liquors, flour, wheat, corn, rice, sugar, molasses or syrup, salt, bacon, pork, hogs, beef or beef cattle, sheep, oats, hay, fodder, raw hides, leather, horses, mules, boots, shoes, cotton yarns, wool, woolen, cotton or mixed cloths, hats, wagons, harness, coal, iron, steel or nails, at any time between the first of January, eighteen hundred and sixty-three, and the first of January eighteen hundred and sixty-five, ten per cent., in addition to the tax on such profits as income under the "act to lay taxes for the common defence, and carry on the Government of the Confederate States," approved April twenty-fourth, eighteen hundred and sixty-three.

II. On all profits made by buying and selling money, gold, silver, foreign exchange, stocks, notes, debts, credits, or obligations of any kind, and any merchandize, property or effects of any kind, not enumerated in the preceding paragraph, between the times named therein, ten per cent., in addition to the tax on such profits as income, under the act aforesaid.

III. On the amount of profits exceeding twenty-five per cent., made during either of the years eighteen hundred and sixty-three and eighteen hundred and sixty-four, by any bank or banking company, insurance, canal, navigation, importing and exporting, telegraph, express, railroad, manufacturing, dry dock, or other joint stock company of any description, whether incorporate or not, twenty-five per cent. on such excess.

Sec. 5. The following exemptions from taxation under this act shall be allowed, to wit:

I. Property of each head of a family to the value of five hundred dollars; and for each minor child of the family to the further value of one hundred dollars; and for each son actually engaged in the army or navy, or who has died or been killed in the military or naval service, and who was a member of the family when he entered the service, to the further value of five hundred dollars.

II. Property of the widow of any officer, soldier, sailor or marine, who may have died or been killed in the military or naval service, or where there is no widow, then of the family, being minor children, to the value of one thousand dollars.

III. Property of every officer, soldier, sailor or marine, actually engaged in the military or naval service, or of such as have been disabled in such service, to the value of one thousand dollars, *Provided*, That the above exemptions shall not apply to any person, whose property, exclusive of household furniture, shall be assessed at a value exceeding one thousand dollars.

IV. That where property has been injured or destroyed by the enemy, or the owner thereof has been temporarily deprived of the use or occupancy thereof, or of the means of cultivating the same, by reason of the presence or the proximity of the enemy, the assessment on such property may be reduced, in proportion to the damage sustained by the owner, or the tax assessed thereon may be reduced in the same ratio by the district collector, on satisfactory evidence submitted to him by the owner or assessor.

Sec. 6. That the taxes on property laid for the year eighteen hundred and sixty-four, shall be assessed as on the day of the passage of this act, and be due and collected on the first day of June next, or as soon after as practicable, allowing an extension of ninety days West of the Mississippi river. The additional taxes on incomes or profits for the year eighteen hundred and sixty-three, levied by this act, shall be assessed and collected forthwith; and the taxes on incomes or profits for the year eighteen hundred and sixty-four, shall be assessed and collected according to the provisions of the tax and assessment acts of eighteen hundred and sixty-three.

Repealed & amended June 14 Sec 8.-

Sec. 7. So much of the tax act of the twenty-fourth day of April, eighteen hundred and sixty-three, as levies a tax on incomes derived from property or effects on the amount or value of which a tax is levied by this act, and also the first section of said act, are suspended for the year eighteen hundred and sixty-four, and no estimated rent, hire or interest on property or credits herein taxed *ad valorem*, shall be assessed or taxed as incomes under the tax act of eighteen hundred and sixty-three.

Sec. 8. That the tax imposed by this act on bonds of the Confederate States heretofore issued, shall in no case exceed the interest on the same, and such bonds, when held by or for minors or lunatics, shall be exempt from the tax in all cases where the interest on the same shall not exceed one thousand dollars.

Approved February 17, 1864.

June 14. 1864

AN ACT TO AMEND THE TAX LAWS.

The Congress of the Confederate States of America do enact, That the first, second, and third sections of the act to levy additional taxes for the common defence and support of the Government, approved 17th of February, 1864, be amended and re-enacted so as to read as follows, to-wit:

SECTION 1. That in addition to the taxes levied by the "Act to lay taxes for the common defence, and to carry on the Government of the Confederate States," approved April 24th, 1863, there shall be levied, from the 17th day of February, 1864, on the subjects of taxation, hereinafter mentioned, and collected from every person, copartnership association or corporation, liable therefor, taxes as follows, to-wit:

I. Upon the value of all property, real, personal, and mixed, of every kind and description, not hereinafter exempted or taxed at a different rate, five per cent: Provided, That from the tax on the value of property employed in agriculture shall be deducted the value of kind derived therefrom during the same year, as assessed under the law imposing it, and delivered to the Government, whether delivered during the year or afterwards including the bacon delivered after, and not prior to, the assessment of the tax on property employed in agriculture, as aforesaid; and the collection of the tax on such property shall be suspended after assessment, under the order of the Secretary of the Treasury, until the value of the tithe to be deducted can be ascertained, and when so ascertained, it shall be the duty of the post quartermaster to certify, and of the district collector to deduct the value of such tithe, and any balance found due may be paid in bonds and certificates therefor, authorized by the "Act to reduce the currency and to authorize a new issue of notes and bonds," in like manner as other taxes, payable during the year: Provided, That no credit shall be allowed beyond five per cent.

II. On the value of gold and silver ware and plate, jewels, jewelry, and watches, ten per cent.

III. The value of property taxed under this section shall be assessed on the basis of the market value of the same, or similar property in the neighborhood where assessed, in the year 1860, except in cases where lands, slaves, cotton, and tobacco have been purchased since the 1st day of January, 1862, in which case the said land, slaves, cotton, and tobacco so purchased, shall be assessed at the price actually paid for the same by the owner: Provided, That land purchased by refugees, and held and occupied by them for their own use and residence, shall be assessed according to the market value in the year 1860.

SEC. 2. That section second of an act entitled "An act to levy additional taxes for the common defence and support of the Government," approved 17th of February, 1864, be, and the same is hereby repealed; and it is hereby declared that all the property and assets of corporations, associations, and joint stock companies, of every description, whether incorporated or not, shall be assessed and taxed in the same manner, and to the same extent, as the property and assets of individuals; the tax on such property and assets, to be assessed against, and paid by such corporations, associations, and joint stock companies: Provided, That no bank or banking company shall be liable to pay a tax upon deposits of money to the credit of and subject to the checks of others; Provided further, That the stock, shares, or interests, representing property or assets in corporations or joint stock companies or associations, shall not be assessed or taxed. And, provided further, That all property within the enemy's lines be, and the same is hereby exempted from all taxation so long as it remains in the enemy's lines.

SEC. 3. That paragraph one, of section three, of an act entitled "An act to levy additional taxes for the common defence and support of the Government," approved 17th February, 1864, be, and the same is hereby amended and re-enacted so as to read as follows: Upon the amount of all gold and silver coin, gold dust, gold or silver bullion, moneys held abroad, or bills of exchange drawn therefor, promissory notes, rights, credits, and securities, payable in foreign countries, five per cent. to be paid in specie, or Confederate Treasury Notes at their value as compared with specie at the time the tax is payable; the relative value of specie and Confederate Treasury Notes, for the purpose of payment under this act, to be fixed by regulations to be prescribed by the Commissioner of Taxes, under the direction of the Secretary of the Treasury.

SEC. 4. That section sixteen, of the "Act to amend an act entitled 'An act to levy taxes for the common defence, and carry on the Government of the Confederate States,' approved 17th February, 1864," be, and the same is hereby, amended so as to read as follows:

I. The income, property, and money, other than Confederate Treasury Notes, of hospitals, asylums, churches, schools, colleges, and other charitable institutions, shall be exempted from taxation under the provisions of this act, or any other law. The property of companies formed under the act entitled "An act to establish a volunteer navy," shall be exempt from taxation, except on the income.

II. That paragraph six, section seven, of the same act, be, and the same is hereby amended by adding thereto, as follows:

"If any person shall fail to make due return, as required by said section, of the income or profits taxed under any law of Congress, or in case of disagreement with the assessor to submit the same to referees, as provided by law, or shall fail or refuse to pay the tax thereon, within such time as shall be prescribed by public notice, by the district collector, under the direction of the Commissioner of Taxes, such person shall be deemed and held to be in default; Provided, That such person shall not be deemed and held to be in default; who may fail, or has failed to make payment, or due returns in consequence of the presence or interference of the enemy, or the absence or neglect of the officers charged with the assessment and collection of taxes."

SEC. 5. That this act shall not be so construed as to subject to taxation, corn, bacon, and other agricultural products, which were produced in the year 1863, and in the possession of the producer on the 17th February, 1864, and necessary for the support of himself and family during the present year, and from or on which taxes in kind have been deducted and delivered or paid.

SEC. 6. That section four, paragraphs one and two, of the act approved 17th February, 1864, entitled "An act to levy additional taxes for the common defence and support of the government," be so amended as to levy an additional tax of thirty per cent. upon the amount of all profits made by selling the articles mentioned in the said paragraphs between the 17th day of February, 1864, and the first day of July next, which additional tax shall be collected under said act.

SEC. 7. That on all Treasury notes of the old issue, of the denomination of five dollars, not exchanged for new issue prior to the 1st day of January, 1865, and which may remain outstanding on that day, a tax of one hundred per cent. is hereby imposed.

SEC. 8. That section seven of an act entitled "An act to levy additional taxes for the common defence and support of the government," approved 17th February, 1864, be, and the same is hereby repealed, and the following inserted in lieu thereof:

I. That the first section of the "Act to levy taxes for the common defence and to carry on the government of the Confederate States," approved 24th April, 1863, is suspended for the year 1864.

II. In all cases where a tax is levied on income derived from property, real, personal, and mixed of every description, on the amount or value of which an *ad valorem* tax is laid, the *ad valorem* tax shall be deducted from the income tax: *Provided*, That in no case shall less be paid than the *ad valorem* tax.

III. In the assessment of income derived from manufacturing or mining, there shall be deducted from the gross income or profits, the necessary annual repairs, not exceeding ten per cent. on the amount of the income derived therefrom. And, in addition to the deductions now allowed by law in the assessment of incomes derived, from any source, the following shall be made, namely: The Confederate taxes actually paid by the owner on sales made by him, and the commissions actually paid by the consignor or shipper for selling, and in the production or manufacture of pig metal, or other iron, the cost of fuel.

SEC. 9. That all citizens of any one of the Confederate States, temporarily residing in another State, shall be liable to be assessed and taxed in the State or district in which he may temporarily reside, and it shall be the duty of all such who have not heretofore made return of their taxable property to the district assessor where they may temporarily reside, within thirty days after the passage of this act, to make such return, and any one liable to be assessed and taxed as aforesaid, who shall fail or refuse, within the said period of thirty days to make such return, shall be liable to all the pains and penalties imposed by the laws of the Confederate States in such case.

Approved June 14, 1864

AN ACT, to amend so much of section eleven of the tax law, as requires one tenth of the sweet potatoes produced this year to be paid to the Government.

The Congress of the Confederate States of America do enact, That so much of section eleven of "An act to lay taxes for the common defence, and carry on the Government of the Confederate States," approved April twenty fourth, eighteen hundred and sixty-three, as requires farmers and planters to pay one tenth of the sweet potatoes produced in the present year to the Confederate Government, be so amended as to authorize the producers of sweet potatoes in the year eighteen hundred and sixty-three, to make commutation, by payment of the money value of the tithe thereof, instead of payment in kind, at rates to be fixed by the commissioners under the impressment act.

Approved December 28th, 1863.

AN ACT for the relief of tax payers in certain cases.

The Congress of the Confederate States of America do enact, That when cotton or other property subject to taxation in money, shall have been burned or otherwise destroyed, by authority of the Government, before the expiration of the time fixed by law, for the payment of the tax thereon, the tax payer may apply to the district collector, who shall investigate the facts and make report thereof to the State collector, who may, if satisfied of such destruction by Government authority, remit the said tax. If the tax in any such case, shall have been paid in advance, it shall be refunded by the State collector. The tax payer shall in every such case, have the right of appeal to the Secretary of the Treasury.

SECTION 2. That in all cases where the crop, out of which the tax in kind is to be paid has been taken or destroyed by the enemy, the district collector may remit the tax, in whole or in part, according to the extent of the loss sustained by the tax payer: *Provided*, That the facts in each case shall be reported to the tax collector, and the remission shall not be valid, until approved by him, *And provided further*, That in case the loss be sustained prior to assessment, the assessor, on satisfactory proof thereof may make deduction therefor in proportion to the loss.

amended June 10. 64 including slaves. –

Approved February 13th, 1864.

AN ACT to be entitled an act in relation to the qualifications of State Collectors.

The Congress of the Confederate States of America do enact, That the provisions of section thirty-nine, of an act entitled "An act for the assessment and collection of taxes," approved May 1, 1863, shall not be construed to apply to the office of State collector.

Approved February 17th, 1864.

Joint Resolution explanatory of the act entitled "An act to lay taxes for the common defence, and carry on the Government," approved the twenty-fourth day of April, eighteen hundred and sixty-three.

Resolved by the Congress of the Confederate States of America, That the daily wages of detailed soldiers, and other employees of the Government, are not liable to taxation as income, although they may amount in the aggregate to the sum of one thousand dollars per annum.

Approved February 17th 1864.

AN ACT authorizing the tax in kind on bacon to be commuted by collection of salt pork as an equivalent.

The Congress of the Confederate States of America do enact, That Assistant Quartermaster's, and other agents, engaged in the collection of tax in kind, may be authorized, under orders and regulations made by the Secretary of War, to demand and receive in commutation for the tax in kind on bacon, an equivalent therefor, in salt pork.

Approved December 28th, 1863.

AN ACT to regulate the collection of the tax in kind upon tobacco, and to amend an act entitled "An act to lay taxes for the common defence, and carry on the Government of the Confederate States," approved April twenty-fourth. eighteen hundred and sixty three.

The Congress of the Confederate States of America do enact, That the tax in kind of one-tenth, imposed by said act, upon all tobacco grown in the Confederate States, instead of being collected by the Post Quartermaster, shall be collected by the agents appointed by the Secretary of the Treasury to collect and preserve tobacco, and the tax assessor shall transfer their estimates of the tobacco due from each planter or farmer, specifying both quantity and quality, to the said agents, or their duly authorized sub-agents, taking their receipts therefor, and shall also transmit a copy of these estimates to the Chief of the Produce Loan Office, and when said tobacco has been collected, the said agent shall be liable for its safe custody.

Sec. 2. That each farmer and planter, not earlier than the first day of June, nor later than the fifteenth day of July, shall deliver his tithe of tobacco in prizing order, put up in convenient parcels for transportation, at the nearest prizing depot, of which there shall be not less than one established in each county, by the agents for the collection and preservation of tobacco, where the said tobacco shall be prized, and securely packed in hogsheads, or other packages, suitable for market, by said agents.

Sec. 3. That the tax assessor shall require a statement from each farmer or planter, as to the different qualities of tobacco raised by him, and shall assess as due the Confederate States, one tenth of each of said qualities, which shall be stated separately in his estimates, and shall be delivered separately by the farmer or planter, at the prizing depots.

Sec. 4. All acts and parts of acts, inconsistent with the foregoing, are hereby repealed.

Approved January 30th, 1864.

THE ASSESSMENT ACT.

AN ACT for the Assessment and Collection of Taxes.

OFFICE OF COMMISSIONER OF TAXES CREATED.

SECTION 1. *The Congress of the Confederate States of America do enact,* That for the purpose of superintending the collection of internal duties, or taxes imposed, or which may be hereafter imposed by law, and of assessing the same, an office is hereby created in the Treasury Department to be called the office of the commissioner of taxes; and the President of the Confederate States is hereby authorized to nominate, and with the advice and consent of the Senate, to appoint a commissioner of taxes, with an annual salary of three thousand dollars, who shall be charged, under the direction of the Secretary of the Treasury, with preparing all the instructions, regulations, directions, forms and blanks, and distributing the same, or any part thereof, and with all other matters pertaining to the assessment and collection of the duties and taxes which may be necessary to carry the laws, passed for the purpose, into effect, and with the general superintendence of his office, as aforesaid, and the Secretary of the Treasury may assign to the office of commissioner of taxes such number of clerks as he may deem necessary, or the exigencies of the public service may require.

Office of commissioner of taxes created.

Commissioner, how appointed. Salary. Duties.

Clerical force.

SEC. 2. That for the purpose of assessing, levying and collecting all taxes and internal duties, each State shall constitute a tax division, over which shall be appointed by the President, with the advice and consent of the Senate, one State collector, who shall be a resident and freeholder in such State, with a salary of one-tenth of one per cent. on the amount collected in each State: *Provided,* That in no case shall the salary be less than two thousand nor more than three thousand dollars, and said State collector shall, under the regulations prescribed by the commissioner of taxes, under the direction of the Secretary of the Treasury, be charged with the duties imposed upon himself, and with the superintendence and direction of all the duties of the various officers in his division or State, created by this act. The said State collector shall give bond, with sureties, to discharge the duties of his office in such amount as may be prescribed by the Secretary of the Treasury, and shall take oath faithfully to discharge the duties of his office and to support and defend the Constitution of the Confederate States.

Each State to constitute a tax division.

State collectors, how appointed. Salary.

Limitations of salaries. Five amended July 17. 64-p. 37

Duties of State collector.

State collectors shall give bond.

Oath of office.

TAX DISTRICTS AND DISTRICT COLLECTORS.

SEC. 3. Each State collector shall divide his State into convenient collection districts, following as nearly as may be practicable the counties or tax districts into which the State may have been sub-divided by

Sub-division of States into collection districts; how regulated.

its own State government. But the Secretary of the Treasury may authorize two or more sparsely populated counties to be included in one collection district, when so recommended by the State collector, and may sub-divide large towns or cities into two or more collection districts, when so recommended by said State collector. For each of these districts a tax collector, to be called the district

District collector how appointed.

collector, shall be appointed by the State collector, subject to the approval of the Secretary of the Treasury, and each of these district collectors shall be charged with the duty of causing to be assessed and

Duties of district collectors.

levied, and of collecting all taxes imposed or required to be paid by any act of Congress, upon any persons or property within the said district. The said district collector shall be a resident freeholder of the tax district in which he shall be appointed, and shall be subject to

Shall be a resident freeholder.

such regulations as shall be prescribed by the commissioner of taxes, under the direction of the Secretary of the Treasury.

SEC. 4. That before any such collector shall enter upon the duties of his office, he shall execute a bond for such amount as shall

District collector shall give bond.

be prescribed by the commissioner of taxes, under the direction of the Secretary of the Treasury, with not less than two sureties, to be approved as sufficient by the commissioner of taxes, conditioned that said collector shall faithfully perform the duties of his office; which bond shall be filed in the office of the Comptroller of the Treasury.

Bond, form and character of.

And each collector shall, from time to time renew, strengthen and increase his official bond, as the Secretary of the Treasury may direct. And each collector, before entering upon the duties of his office, shall

Collector shall renew bond.

take oath faithfully to discharge the duties of his office, and that he will support and defend the Constitution of the Confederate States.

SEC. 5. That each district collector shall be authorized to appoint, by an instrument of writing under his hand, as many deputies as he

Collector's oath of office.

may think proper, to be by him compensated for their services, and also to revoke any such appointment, giving such notice thereof as the commissioner of taxes shall prescribe; and may require bonds, or

District collectors may appoint deputies.

Compensation of deputies.

District collectors may revoke appointment of deputies, and may require bonds and security.

Deputies, authority of.

other securities, and accept the same from such deputy; and each such deputy shall have the like authority in every respect, to collect the duties and taxes levied and assessed within the portion of the district assigned to him, which is by this act vested in the district collector himself; but each district collector shall, in every respect, be responsible for all monies collected, and for every act done as deputy collector by any of his deputies whilst acting as such, and for every omission of duty. The collector in each State shall appoint in each district, subject to the approval of the Secretary of the Treasury, an

District collector responsible for deputies.

assessor or assessors, who shall be residents therein, and each assessor so appointed and accepting the appointment, shall, before he enters on the duties of his appointment, take and subscribe, before some com-

Assessors, how appointed.

petent magistrate, or some district collector to be appointed by virtue of this act, (who is hereby empowered to administer the same) the following oath or affirmation, to-wit: "*I, A. B., do swear, or af-*

Assessor shall take oath of office.

firm, (as the case may be,) *that I will support the Constitution of the Confederate States of America, and that I will, to the best of my know-*

Assessor's oath.

ledge, skill and judgment, diligently and faithfully execute the office and duties of assessor for (naming the district) *without favor or parti-*

Certificate of oath to be given to collector.

ality, and that I will do equal right and justice in every case in which I shall act as assessor." And a certificate of such oath or affirmation shall be delivered to the collector of the district for which such assessor shall be appointed. And every assessor acting in the said office without having taken the said oath or affirmation, shall forfeit and pay one hundred dollars, one moiety thereof to the use of the Confederate States, and the other moiety thereof to him who shall first sue for the same, with costs of suit: *Provided*, That nothing herein contained shall prevent any district collector from collecting himself the whole or any part of the duties and taxes so assessed and payable in his district.

Penalty for failure to make oath.

District collector not prevented from collecting all duties, &c.

RETURNS TO ASSESSORS. DUTY OF TAX PAYERS THEREIN.

SEC. 6. That it shall be the duty of any person or persons, partnerships, firms, associations, or corporations, made liable to any tax, imposed by any act imposing taxes, at the time prescribed by law, or if no time be fixed by law, then at such times as may be prescribed by the commissioner of taxes, under the direction of the Secretary of the Treasury, to make, under oath or affirmation, as the case may be, a list or return to the assessor of the district where located, of the amount of annual income or profits, the articles or objects charged with a special tax, the quantity of goods, wares and merchandize made or sold, and charged with a specific or *ad valorem* tax, the market value of the property, real and personal, charged with an *ad valorem* tax, the several rates and aggregate amounts, and all other matters and things which are or shall be required by law, and according to the forms and regulations to be prescribed by the commissioner of taxes, under the direction of the Secretary of the Treasury, for which such person or persons, partnerships, firms, associations or corporations are or shall be liable to be assessed according to law.

Tax-payers to make returns under oath to assessor.

Returns, character of.

SEC. 7. That the instructions, regulations and directions, as hereinbefore mentioned, shall be binding on each assessor and on each collector and his deputy or deputies, in the performance of the duties enjoined by or under this act; pursuant to which instructions the district collector shall direct and cause the several assessors to proceed through every part of their respective districts, and inquire after and concerning all persons being within the collection districts where they repectively reside, owning, possessing, or having the care and management of any property, goods, wares and merchandise, articles or objects liable to pay any tax, (by reference as well to any list of assessment or collection taken under the laws of the respective States, as to any other records or documents, and by all other lawful ways and means, especially to the written list, schedule or return required to be made to the assessor by all persons, owning, possessing, or having the care or management of any property as aforesaid, liable to taxation,) and to value and enumerate the said objects of taxation respectively, in the manner prescribed by law, and in conformity with the regulations and instructions before mentioned.

Instructions, &c to be binding on all officers.

Assessments, how to be made.

DUTY OF ASSESSOR WHERE PERSON FAILS TO EXHIBIT LIST.

SEC. 8. That if any person owning, possessing, or having the care or management of property, goods, wares and merchandise, articles or objects liable to pay any tax, shall fail to make and exhibit a written list when required, as aforesaid, and shall consent to disclose the particulars of any and all the property, goods, wares and merchandise, articles and objects liable to pay any tax, or any business or occupation liable to pay any tax, as aforesaid, then, and in that case, it shall be the duty of the officer to make such list, which, being distinctly read, consented to, and signed by the person so owning, possessing, or having the care and management, as aforesaid, shall be received as the list of such person.

List to be made by assessor in case of failure of tax payer to make list.

FALSE OR FRAUDULENT LIST.

Fraudulent or false list, penalty for making.

SEC. 9. That if any person shall deliver or disclose to any assessor appointed in pursuance of this act, and requiring a list or lists, as aforesaid, any false or fraudulent list or statement, with intent to defeat or evade the valuation or enumeration hereby intended to be made, such person so offending, and being thereof convicted, on indictment found therefor in any district court of the Confederate States, held in the district in which such offence may be committed, shall be fined in a sum not exceeding five hundred dollars, at the discretion of the court, and shall pay all costs and damages of prosecution; and the valuation and enumeration required by this act, shall, in all such cases, and in all cases of under-valuation or under-statement in such lists or statements, be made as aforesaid, upon lists according to the form prescribed, to be made out by the assessors respectively; which lists, the said assessors are hereby authorized and required to make, according to the best information they can obtain, and for the purpose of making which, they are hereby authorized to enter into and upon all and singular the premises respectively.

How prosecuted.

Valuation, how made in case of fraudulent return.

Assessor authorized to enter upon premises, &c.

DUTY OF ASSESSOR, IN CASE OF REFUSAL TO MAKE RETURN, AND PENALTY.

Assessor to enter premises and make list.

SEC. 10. That if any person shall refuse or neglect to give such list or lists within the time required as aforesaid, it shall be the duty of the assessor for the collection district within which such person shall reside, and he is hereby authorized and required to enter into and upon the premises, if it be necessary, of such person so refusing or neglecting, and to make, according to the best information which he can obtain, or on his own view and information, such lists of property, goods, wares, and merchandise, and of all articles and objects liable to taxation, owned or possessed, or under the care or management of such person, as are required by law, including the amount, if any, due upon a registered business; and in case of refusal or neglect, to make such lists, except in cases of sickness, or other unavoidable cause, the assessor shall thereupon, except where otherwise provided for, add twenty-five per centum to the amount of the items thereof; and the lists so made and subscribed by such assessor, shall be taken and reported as good and sufficient lists of the persons and property for which such person or property is to be taxed for the purposes of this act.

Penalty for failure to make list.

List shall be accepted,

IN REFERENCE TO PROPERTY WHEN THE OWNER RESIDES OUT OF DISTRICT.

SEC. 11. That whenever there shall be in any collection district, any property, goods, wares and merchandise, articles or objects, not owned or possessed by, or under the care or management of, any person or persons within such district, and liable to be taxed as aforesaid, and no list of which shall have been transmitted to the assessor in the manner provided by this act, it shall be the duty of the assessor for such district, and he is hereby authorized and required to enter into and upon the premises where such property is situated, and take such views thereof as may be necessary, and to make lists of the same, according to the form prescribed, which lists, being subscribed by the said assessor, shall be taken and reputed as good and sufficient lists of such property, goods, wares and merchandise, articles or objects, as aforesaid, under and for the purpose of this act.

Property of non-resident tax payers.

Assessor to enter premises and make survey and list.

SEC. 12. That the owners, possessors, or persons having the care or management of property, goods, wares and merchandise, articles or objects not lying or being within the collection district in which they reside, shall be permitted to make out and deliver the lists thereof, required by this act, (provided the district in which the said objects of duty or taxation are situated is therein distinctly stated,) at the time and in the manner prescribed to the assessor of the district wherein such persons reside. And it shall be the duty of the assessor who receives any such list to transmit the same to the assessor where such objects of taxation are situate, who shall examine such lists; and if he approves the same, he shall return it to the assessor from whom he received it, with his approval thereof; and if he fails to approve the same, he shall make such alteration thereon as he may deem to be just and proper, and shall then return the said list, with such alterations thereon, or additions thereto, to the assessor from whom he received the said list; and the assessor where the person liable to pay such tax resides, shall proceed in making the assessment of the tax upon the list by him so received, in all respects, as if the said list had been made out by himself.

Property located in districts outside of that in which the owners reside, may by them be returned to the assessor thereof.

List to be transmitted to the assessor of the district where such property is located.

DISTRICT COLLECTORS, AFTER COLLECTING THE LISTS, SHALL MAKE TWO GENERAL LISTS.

SEC. 13. That the lists aforesaid shall be taken at such times as may be prescribed by the commissioner of taxes under the direction of the Secretary of the Treasury or with reference to the time when said taxes become due; and the district collectors respectively, after collecting the said lists, shall proceed to arrange the same, and to make two general lists, the first of which shall exhibit, in alphabetical order, the names of all persons liable to pay any tax, residing within the collection district, together with the value and assessment, or enumeration, as the case may require, of the objects liable to taxation within such district, for which each such person is liable, or for which any firm, company or corporation is liable, with the amount of tax payable thereon; and the second list shall exhibit, in alphabetical order, the names of all persons residing out of the collection district, owners of property within the district, together with the value and assessment, or enumeration thereof, as the case may be, with the amount of tax payable thereon, as aforesaid. The forms of the said general list shall be devised and prescribed by the State collector, under the direction of the commissioner of taxes, and lists taken according to such forms shall be made out by the assessor or assessors,

Two lists to be made by district collectors.

Lists shall contain names of all tax payers residing within district.

List of tax payers residing out of collection district.

Forms of lists to be made by State collector.

Lists to be delivered to district

collectors. and delivered to the district collector within thirty days after the time fixed by this act as aforesaid. And if any assessor shall fail to perform any duty assigned by this act within the time as aforesaid, not being prevented therefrom by sickness, or other unavoidable cause, every such assessor shall be discharged from office, and shall, moreover, forfeit and pay the sum of two hundred dollars, to be recovered for the use of the Confederate States, with costs of suit.

Penalty for failure of assessor to perform duties of his office.

WHERE LISTS MAY BE EXAMINED, AND WHEN APPEALS SHALL BE TAKEN, DECIDED, ETC.

Time and place of making lists to be advertised.

SEC. 14. The collectors for each collection district shall, by advertisement in some public newspaper published within his district, if any such there be, or by written or printed notifications, to be posted up in at least four places within each district, advertise all persons concerned, of the time and place within said district when and where the lists, valuations and enumerations, made and taken within said district, may be examined; and said lists shall remain open for the space of fifteen days after notice shall have been given as aforesaid. And said notifications shall also state when and where, within said district, after the expiration of said fifteen days, appeals will be received and determined relative to any erroneous or excessive valuation or enumerations by the assessor. And it shall be the duty of each collector for each collection district, at the time fixed for hearing such appeal as aforesaid, to submit the lists taken and returned as aforesaid, to the inspection of any and all persons who may apply for that purpose. And the said collector for each collection district is hereby authorized at any time within fifteen days from and after the time allowed for notification as aforesaid, to hear and determine, in a summary way, according to law and right, upon any and all appeals which may be exhibited: *Provided*, That the question to be determined by the collector, on an appeal respecting the valuation or enumeration of property, or objects liable to taxation shall be, whether the valuation complained of be or be not in a just relation or proportion to other valuations in the same district, and whether the enumeration be or not correct. And all appeals to the district collector, as aforesaid, shall be made in writing, and shall specify the particular cause, matter, or thing respecting which a decision is requested; and shall, moreover, state the ground or principle of inequality or error complained of. And the collector shall have power to re-examine and equalize the valuations as shall appear just and equitable; but no valuation or enumeration shall be increased without a previous notice, of at least five days, to the party interested to appear and object to the same, if he judge proper; which notice shall be given by a note in writing, to be personally served or left at the dwelling house, office, or place of business of the party by such collector: *Provided*, That this section shall not apply to estimates of income and profits, or of taxes in kind, made by appraisers or referees as prescribed in the act passed in April, in the year eighteen hundred and sixty-three, entitled "An act to lay taxes for the common defence and carry on the government of the Confederate States."

Lists shall remain open fifteen days.

Appeals; when and where to be received; notification thereof to be made.

Collector shall submit list to all persons.

Collector to hear and determine appeals.

What question of appeal shall be determined by district collector.

Appeals to be made in writing and what they shall state.

Collector has power to examine and equalize valuations.

Notice of increase in valuation by collector to be given tax payer.

Section not applicable to estimates of income and profits, or of taxes in kind.

THE PREPARATION OF LISTS FOR STATE COLLECTORS AND THE MODE AND MANNER OF COLLECTING TAXES.

SEC. 15. The district collectors shall, immediately after the expiration of the time for hearing and deciding appeals, make out correct lists of the valuation and enumeration in each of their districts respectively, and deliver the same to the State collector, who shall collate the same in proper form and forward the same to the commissioner of taxes.

Lists to be made and forwarded to State collector, who shall collate the same.

SEC. 16. As soon as the said district collectors shall deliver their lists of assessment to the State Collector, they shall respectively give notice, by advertisement published in each collection district, in one newspaper printed in said district, if any such there be, and by notifications to be posted up in at least four public places in each district, that the said taxes have become due and payable, and state the time and place within said district at which he will attend to receive the same, which time shall not be less than thirty days after such notification; and all persons who shall neglect to pay the taxes so assessed as aforesaid, upon them, to the collector within the time specified, shall be liable to pay ten per centum additional upon the amount thereof, the fact of which liability shall be stated in the advertisement and notification aforesaid. And with regard to all persons who shall neglect to pay as aforesaid, it shall be the duty of the collector in person, or by deputy, within twenty days after such neglect to make a demand personally, or at the dwellings or usual places of business of such persons, if any they have, for payment of said taxes, with the ten per cent. additional, aforesaid. And with respect to all such taxes as are not included in the lists aforesaid, and all taxes, the collection of which is not otherwise provided for in this act, it shall be the duty of each collector, in person, or by deputy, to demand payment thereof, in manner aforesaid, within ten days from and after the same become due by law; and if the annual and other taxes shall not be paid within ten days from and after such demand therefor, it shall be lawful for such collector, or his deputy or deputies, to proceed to collect the said taxes by distraint and sale of the goods, chattels, or effects of the persons delinquent as aforesaid. And in case of such distraint, it shall be the duty of the officer charged with the collection to make, or cause to be made, an account of the goods or chattels which may be distrained, a copy of which, signed by the officer making such distraint, shall be left with the owner or possessor of such goods, chattels, or effects, or at his or her dwelling with some person of suitable age and discretion, with a note of the sum demanded, and the time and place of sale; and the said officer shall forthwith cause a notification to be published in some newspaper within the district wherein the distraint is made, if there is a newspaper published in said district, or to be publicly posted up at the postoffice, if there be one within five miles, nearest to the residence of the person whose property shall be distrained, and in not less than two other public places, which notice shall specify the articles distrained and the time and place for sale thereof, which time shall not be less than ten nor more than twenty days from the date of such notification, and the place proposed for sale not more than five miles distant from the place of making such distraint: *Provided*, That in case of distraint for the payment of the taxes aforesaid, the

District collectors shall give notice when taxes are due and payable, with time and place of payment.

Penalty for failure to pay taxes when due.

How collector shall proceed in case of failure to pay taxes.

Collector shall make demand for payment of all taxes not included in lists.

How collector shall proceed in case of failure to pay.

Collector shall distrain.

In case of distraint, an account of goods, &c., shall be made by collector and copy thereof left with tax payer, accompanied by demand for payment, &c.

Notification of distraint to be advertised.

What notice of distraint shall specify.

Distrained goods, when returnable to tax payer.

goods, chattels, or effects so distrained shall and may be restored to the owner or possessor, if, prior to the sale, payment or tender shall be made to the proper officer charged with the collection, of the full amount demanded, together with such fee for levying, and such sum for the necessary and reasonable expense of removing, advertising and keeping the goods, chattels, or effects so distrained, as may be prescribed by the commissioner of taxes; but in case of non-payment or tender as aforesaid, the said officer shall proceed to sell the said goods, chattels, or effects, at public auction, and shall and may retain from the proceeds of such sale, the amount demandable for the use of the Confederate States, with the necessary and reasonable expenses of distraint and sale, and a commission of five per centum thereon for his own use, rendering the over plus, if any there be, to the person whose goods, chattels, or effects, shall have been distrained.

Collector shall sell in case of refusal to pay taxes, and how he is to dispose of the proceeds of sale.

When distrained property is not divisible, how collector shall proceed.

SEC. 17. That in all cases where the property liable to distraint for taxes under any act of Congress, may not be divisible, so as to enable the collector by a sale of part thereof to raise the whole amount of the tax with all costs, charges and commissions, the whole of such property shall be sold, and the surplus of the proceeds of the sale, after satisfying the tax, costs and charges, shall be paid to the owner of the property, or his or their legal representatives, or if he, she or they cannot be found, or refuse to receive the same, then such surplus shall be deposited in the treasury of the Confederate States, in such manner as may be prescribed by the Secretary of the Treasury, to be there set apart and held for the use of the owner, or his or her or their legal representatives, until he, she or they shall make application therefor to the Secretary of the Treasury, who, upon such application, shall, by warrant on the treasury, cause the same to be paid to the applicant. And if the property advertised for sale as aforesaid, cannot be sold for the amount of the tax due thereon, with the costs and charges, the collector shall purchase the same in behalf of the Confederate States for an amount not exceeding the tax, with the costs and charges thereon. And all property so purchased may be sold by said collector, under such regulations as may be prescribed by the commissioner of taxes. And the collector shall render a distinct account of all charges incurred in the sale of such property, and shall pay into the treasury the surplus, if any there be, after defraying the charge.

In case distrained property is insufficient to pay taxes, &c.

Collector shall render account of all charges incurred in sale, and pay over surplus of proceeds.

Statutory lien, taxes shall be a.

SEC. 18. The taxes assessed upon each person shall be a statutory lien upon all property of such person for and during the term of two years from the date of listing such person, in preference to any other lien, and the lands and other property of any collector shall be bound by statutory lien for five years for all monies received by him for taxes, the date of such lien to commence from the time of his receiving the money. And the said liens shall extend to each and every part of all tracts or lots of land or dwelling houses, notwithstanding the same may have been divided or alienated in part.

Property of collectors to be bound by statutory lien.

SALE OF REAL ESTATE AUTHORIZED. WHERE GOODS AND CHATTELS ARE INSUFFICIENT TO SATISFY TAXES.

Collector authorized to seize real estate.

SEC. 19. That in any case where goods, chattels or effects, sufficient to satisfy the taxes imposed by law upon any person liable to pay the same shall not be found by the collector or deputy collector whose duty it may be to collect the same, he is hereby authorized to collect the same by seizure and sale of real estate of such person; and the officers making such seizure and sale shall give notice to the person whose estate is proposed to be sold, by giving him in hand, or leaving at his usual place of abode, a notice in writing, stating what particular estate is proposed to be sold, describing the same with reasonable certainty, and the time, when, and place where, said officer proposes to sell the same. And the said collector shall first advertise the same for thirty days in a newspaper printed within the collection district, if such there be, or shall post up in at least four public places within the district a notification of the intended sale thirty days previous thereto and shall proceed to sell at public sale so much of the said property as may be necessary to satisfy the taxes due, together with an addition of twenty per centum. But in all cases where the property liable to tax under this act may not be divisible so as to enable the collector by a sale of part thereof to raise the whole amount of the tax, with all costs, charges and commissions, the whole of such property shall be sold, and the surplus of the proceeds of the sale, after satisfying the tax, costs, charges and commissions, shall be paid to the owner of the property, or to his legal representatives, or if he or they cannot be found, or refuse to receive the same, then such surplus shall be deposited in the treasury, there to be held and drawn out in like manner as provided in this act in reference to the surplus arising from the sale of goods, chattels and effects. And if the property advertised for sale as aforesaid, cannot be sold for the amount of tax due thereon, with the said additional twenty per centum thereto, the collector shall purchase the same in behalf of the Confederate States for the amount aforesaid: *Provided*, That the owner or superintendent of the property aforesaid, after the same shall have been, as aforesaid, advertised for sale, and before it shall have been actually sold, shall be allowed to pay the amount of the tax thereon, with an addition of ten per centum on the same, on the payment of which the sale of the property shall not take place: *Provided, also*, That the owners, their heirs, executors, or administrators, or any person on their behalf, shall have liberty to redeem the lands and other property sold as aforesaid, within two years from the time of sale, upon payment to the collector for the use of the purchaser, his heirs or assigns, of the amount paid by such purchaser, with interest for the same at the rate of twenty per centum per annum; and no deed shall be given until the time of redemption shall have expired: *Provided further*, That when the owner of any land or other real property sold for taxes under the provisions of this act shall be in the military service of the Confederate States, before and at the time said sale shall have been made, or shall be an infant under twenty-one years of age, a married woman, or person of unsound mind, the said owner shall have the privilege of redeeming the said property at any time within two years after the close of his term of service, or after the disability of such infant, married woman, or person of unsound mind, is removed. And the collector shall render a distinct account of the charges incurred in offering and advertising for sale such property, and shall pay into the treasury the surplus, if any there be, of the aforesaid addition of twenty per centum, or ten per centum, as the case may be, after

Notice of seizure to be given.

Advertisement of seizure to be made.

How collector shall proceed when property is not divisible.

Collector shall sell.

Surplus of proceeds of sale, how to be disposed.

When property advertised for sale is insufficient to pay taxes.

When tax payer shall have power to stop sale.

How and when property sold for taxes may be redeemed.

When tax payer is in the military service of the Confederate States, or an infant, or feme covert, or of unsound mind.

Collector shall render an account of sale, and pay over surplus of proceeds thereof.

Deeds for property sold for taxes, how made.

defraying the charges. And in every case of the sale of real estate, which shall be made under the authority of this act by the collectors respectively, or their lawful deputies respectively, the deeds for the estate so sold shall be prepared, made and executed, and proved or acknowledged, at the time and times prescribed in this act by the collectors respectively, within whose collection district such real estate shall be situated, in such form of law as shall be authorized and required by the laws of the State in which such real estate lies, for making, executing, proving and acknowledging deeds of bargain and sale, or other conveyances for the transfer and conveyance of real estate; and for every deed so prepared, made, executed, proved and acknowledged, the purchaser or grantee shall pay to the collector the sum of two dollars for the use of collector or other person effecting the sale of the real estate thereby conveyed: *Provided*, That all lands sold to one person at the same time shall be included in one deed. It shall be the duty of every collector to keep a record of all sales of land made in his collection district, whether by himself or his deputy, in which shall be set forth the tax for which any such sale was made, the dates of seizure and sale, the name of the party assessed, and all proceedings in making said sale, the amount of fees and expenses, the name of purchaser, and the date of sale, which record shall be certified by the officer making the sale. And it shall be the duty of any deputy making sale as aforesaid to return a statement of all his proceedings to the collector, and to certify the record thereof. This record shall be deposited in the clerk's office of the district court of the Confederate States, in which the lands sold are situate, and a certified copy thereof shall be *prima facie* evidence in any court of the facts stated therein. And when any lands sold as aforesaid shall be redeemed as hereinbefore provided, the collector shall certify the fact of such redemption to the clerk of said court, to be filed with the record aforesaid as evidence of such redemption. And the claim of the government to lands sold under and by virtue of the foregoing provisions, shall be held to have accrued at the time of the seizure thereof.

Purchaser to pay for papers. All lands sold to one person at same time shall be included in one deed. Collector shall keep record of all sales, and what such records shall exhibit. Deputy making sale to return statement thereof under certificate to collector. Record thereof to be made in district court, and to be *prima facie* evidence of the facts stated therein. When lands are redeemed collector shall so certify to the clerk of the court. When claim of the government to lands sold for taxes accrues.

RECEIPTS FOR TAXES AND DISPOSITION OF MONIES COLLECTED.

Collectors shall sign duplicate receipts.

SEC. 20. Upon receiving the tax due by each person, the collector shall sign receipts in duplicate, one whereof shall be delivered to the person paying the same, and the other shall be forwarded to the State collector of that State. The money collected during each month, or during any shorter period which may be designated by the Secretary of the Treasury, shall be also immediately forwarded to the said State collector; and the several State collectors shall, at the expiration of every month after collections have been commenced, transmit to the commissioner of taxes a statement of the amount of collections received within the month, and pay over monthly, or at such time or times as may be required by the commissioner of taxes the monies by them respectively received within the said term, and at such places as may be designated and required by the commissioner of taxes; and each of the district collectors shall complete the collection of all sums annually assigned to them for collection, shall pay over the same to the State collector, and shall render his final account to the said State collector as often as he may be required, and within six months from and after the day when he shall have received the collection lists from

Monies collected for taxes to be forwarded to State collector. State collector shall make monthly returns of receipts to commissioner of taxes and pay over monies when required. District collectors shall complete collections, pay over all monies and render final account whenever required.

the assessor or assessors of his district. And the Secretary of the Treasury is authorized to designate one or more depositories in each State for the deposit and safe keeping of the monies collected by virtue of this act; and the receipt of the proper officer of such depository to a State collector for the money deposited by him shall be a sufficient voucher for such State collector in the settlement of his accounts at the Treasury Department; and the commissioner of taxes may, under the direction of the Secretary of the Treasury, prescribe such regulations with reference to such deposits as he may deem necessary. And the State collector shall furnish the commissioner of taxes with a list specifying the names and amounts of each of the tax receipts which shall have been forwarded to him as aforesaid by the district collectors.

Depositories: Secretary of the Treasury to designate for safe keeping of monies.

Receipt of depositary to be voucher for State collector.

Regulations for deposit to be prescribed by commissioner of taxes.

State collector to furnish commissioner of taxes with lists containing names and amounts of tax receipts.

SEC. 21. That each collector shall be charged with the whole amount of taxes, whether contained in the lists delivered to him by the assessors respectively, or delivered or transmitted to him by other collectors, and shall be credited with the amount of taxes contained in the lists transmitted in the manner above provided to other collectors, and by him receipted as aforesaid, and also for the taxes of such persons as may have absconded or become insolvent prior to the day when the tax ought, according to the provisions of this act, to have been collected: *Provided*, That it shall be proved to the satisfaction of the comptroller of the Treasury, that due diligence was used by the collector, and that no property was left from which the tax could have been recovered. And each collector shall also be credited with the amount of property purchased by him for the use of the Confederate States, provided he shall faithfully account for and pay over the proceeds thereof upon a resale of the same as required by this act.

Collector charged with whole amount of taxes.

Collector how credited.

Comptroller of Treasury shall be satisfied that due diligence was employed by collector.

Property purchased for Confederate States to be credited to collector.

DEFAULTING COLLECTORS. DISTRESS WARRANT AGAINST THEM AND THEIR SURETIES.

SEC. 22. That if any collector shall fail to collect or pay over to the chief collector, the amounts collected as hereinbefore provided, it shall be the duty of the State collector, and he is hereby authorized and required, immediately after such delinquency, to report the same to the commissioner of taxes, who shall issue a warrant of distress against such delinquent collector and his sureties, directed to the marshal of the district, therein expressing the amount of the taxes with which the said collector is chargeable and the sums, if any, which have been paid. And the said marshal shall himself, or by his deputy, immediately proceed to levy and collect the sum which may remain due, by distress and sale of the goods and chattels, or any personal effects of the delinquent collector, giving at least five days notice of the time and place of sale, in the manner provided by law for advertising sales of personal property on execution in the State wherein such collector resides: *And, furthermore*, If such goods, chattels and effects cannot be found sufficient to satisfy the said warrant, the said marshal or his deputy shall and may proceed to levy and collect the sum which remains due, by distress and sale of goods and chattels, or personal effects of the surety or sureties of the delinquent collector, giving notice as hereinbefore provided. And the bill of sale of the officer of any goods, chattels or other personal property, distrained and sold as aforesaid, shall be *prima facie* evidence of title to the purchaser, and of the right of the

State collector to report delinquent district collectors.

Commissioner of taxes shall issue warrant of distress.

Marshal shall levy and collect by distress and sale, after giving notice thereof.

In case goods of collector are insufficient to satisfy warrant, how marshal shall proceed.

Bill of sale of marshal to be *prima facie* evidence of title to purchaser.

Lands and real estate of collector and sureties to be distrained in case personal effects are insufficient to satisfy warrant of distress.

officer to make such sale, and of the correctness of his proceedings in selling the same. And for want of goods and chattels, or other personal effects of such collector or his sureties, sufficient to satisfy any warrant of distress, issued pursuant to the preceding section of this act, the lands and real estate as such collector and sureties, or so much thereof as may be necessary for satisfying the said warrant, after being advertised for at least three weeks in not less than three public places in the collection district, and in one newspaper printed in the district, if any there be, prior to the proposed time of sale, may and shall be sold at public auction by the marshal or his deputy, who, upon such sale, shall, as such marshal or deputy marshal, make and deliver to the purchaser of the premises so sold a deed of conveyance thereof, to be executed and acknowledged in manner and form prescribed by the laws of the State in which said lands are situated, which said deed so made shall invest the purchaser with all the title and interest of the defendant or defendants named in said warrant, existing at the time of seizure thereof, and all monies that remain of the proceeds of such sale, after satisfying the said warrant of distress, and paying the reasonable costs and charges of sale, shall be returned to the proprietor of the lands or real estate sold as aforesaid.

Marshal to make and deliver deed of conveyance.

Surplus of proceeds of sale, after paying costs, &c., to be paid over to proprietors of land.

EXTORTION AND PENALTY THEREOF.

SEC. 23. That each and every collector or his deputy, who shall exercise or be guilty of any extortion or wilful oppression under color of this act, or shall knowingly demand other or greater sums than shall be authorized by this act, shall be liable to pay a sum not exceeding double the amount of damages accruing to the party injured, to be recovered by and for the use of the party injured, with costs of suit, and shall be dismissed from office, and be disqualified from holding such office thereafter; and each and every collector or his deputy shall give receipts for all sums by them collected and retained in pursuance of this act.

Penalty for extortion by collector.

Collectors and deputies shall give receipts for all collections.

SEC. 24. That all property, credits, income and profits, and every article or object subjected to taxation, shall be estimated, valued and assessed, at the value thereof at the time of assessment, in Confederate notes.

Estimate and valuation of property, credits, &c., how to be made.

COLLECTORS AND ASSESSORS TO ENTER BUILDING. PENALTY FOR REFUSING TO ADMIT THEM.

SEC. 25. That the collector or deputy collector or assessor shall be authorized to enter, in the day time, any brewery, distillery, manufactory, building, or place other than the dwelling house, where any property, articles or objects subject to taxation are made, produced or kept within his district, or in which any taxed business is conducted, so far as it may be necessary to ascertain the amount and value of said property, articles or objects, he may also inspect any books in which are kept the entries of such items as are required to make the returns required from time to time to be made; and every owner of such brewery, distillery, manufactory, building or place, other than the dwelling house, or persons having the agency or superintendence of the same, who shall refuse to admit such officer, or to suffer him to examine said property, articles or objects, or to inspect said accounts, shall for every such refusal, forfeit and pay the sum of five hundred dollars.

Collectors, deputies and assessors to have right of entry to all premises except dwelling houses.
To inspect books.

Penalty for refusal to admit collectors, etc.

COLLECTOR BEING SICK DEPUTY TO ACT.

SEC. 26. That in case of the sickness or temporary disability of a collector to discharge such of his duties as cannot, under existing laws be discharged by a deputy, they may be devolved by him on his deputy: *Provided*, That information thereof be immediately communicated to the Secretary of the Treasury, and shall not be disapproved by him: *And provided further*, That the responsibility of the collector or his sureties to the Confederate States shall not be affected or impaired thereby.

Deputy authorized to act as collector in case of sickness of latter.

Information thereof to be forwarded Secretary of Treasury.

Collector to be responsible.

DEATH OF COLLECTOR.

SEC. 27. That in case a collector shall die, the deputy of such collector, if he have one, shall continue to act until the successor be appointed: *Provided*, He shall not so act for a period exceeding sixty days; and the deputy of such collector may and shall, until a successor shall be appointed, discharge all the duties of said collector; and for the official acts and defaults of such deputy, a remedy shall be had on the official bond of the collector, as in other cases; and any bond or security taken of such deputy by such collector, pursuant to the provisions in this act, shall be available to his heirs or representatives, to indemnify them for loss or damage accruing from any act of the proper deputy so continuing or so succeeding to the duties of such collector.

Deputy to act in case of collector's death.

How long deputy shall act.

Remedy to be had on official bond of collector in case of default of deputy.

Bond of deputy to be available to heirs of collector in case of default of former.

COLLECTORS AND DEPUTIES AUTHORIZED TO COLLECT ALL TAXES, AND PROSECUTE FOR RECOVERY OF FINES AND PENALTIES.

SEC. 28. That it shall be the duty of the collectors aforesaid, or their deputies, in their respective districts, and they are hereby authorized to collect all the taxes imposed by law, however the same may be designated, and to prosecute for the recovery of the same, and for the recovery of any sum or sums which may be forfeited by virtue of this act; and all fines, penalties and forfeitures which may be incurred or imposed by virtue of this act, shall and may be sued for and recovered in the name and for the use of the Confederate States, in any proper form of action or proceeding, before any court of competent jurisdiction: *Provided*, That any person who is a non-resident of the State in which he may have taxes to pay, may pay the whole amount of such taxes directly to the State collector of the State in which such taxes are due, and any person having to pay taxes in two or more collection districts of the same State, may, if he resides in such State, pay the whole amount of his taxes in that State to the district collector of the district wherein the tax-payer resides, and the said State or district collector, as the case may be, shall issue separate receipts, in duplicate, to such tax-payer, for the amount of taxes due and paid on property in each collection district where the same is located, one of said receipts to be retained by the tax-payer and the other to be delivered to the district collector of the district in which the property designated therein is situated.

Fines, penalties, etc., to be recovered in the name and for the use of the Confederate States.

Non resident tax-payers may pay whole amount of taxes to State collector of State where property is located.

Tax-payers may pay taxes due on property located within two or more collection districts to collector of district wherein they reside.

Duplicate to receipts to be given such tax payers, one to be retained by them and the other delivered to collector of district where property therein designated is situated.

FALSE SWEARING HELD AS PERJURY. PENALTIES THEREOF.

SEC. 20. Oaths and affirmations required under this act, may be administered by any collector or assessor; and if any person, in any

Oaths may be administered by collector or assessor. case, matter, hearing or other proceeding, in which an oath or affirmation shall be required to be taken or administered under and by virtue of this act, shall, upon the taking of such oath or affirmation, knowingly and willingly swear or affirm falsely, every person so offending shall be deemed guilty of perjury, and shall on conviction thereof, be subject to the like punishment and penalties now provided by the laws of the Confederate States for the crime of perjury.

False swearing deemed perjury.

Penalty for false swearing.

ACCOUNTS TO BE KEPT AT TREASURY OF MONIES RECEIVED FROM EACH STATE. IN CASE OF LEVY AND SALE PARTY AGGRIEVED TO APPLY TO COLLECTOR FOR RELIEF.

SEC. 30. That separate accounts shall be kept at the Treasury of all monies received from each of the respective States, and the State collector shall procure from each tax collector such details as to the tax, and shall classify the same in such manner as the Secretary of the Treasury shall direct, and so as to provide full information as to each subject of taxation.

State collector to specify details of tax.

Remedy for taxpayers applying for relief.

SEC. 31. That when any tax shall have been paid by levy and distraint, any person or persons, or party who may feel aggrieved thereby may apply to the district collector for relief, and exhibit such evidence as he, she or they may have of the wrong done or supposed to have been done, and after a full investigation the collector shall report the case, with such parts of the evidence as he may judge material, including, also, such as may be regarded material by the party aggrieved, to the State collector, and the State collector shall, if it be made to appear to him that such tax was levied or collected, in whole or in part, wrongfully or unjustly, refund the amount, and shall have credit therefor at the Treasury.

District collector to forward evidence in the case to State collector. State collector may refund am'ts when considered wrongfully levied.

BILL OF SALE PRIMA FACIE EVIDENCE OF COLLECTOR'S RIGHT TO SELL GOODS, ETC.

SEC. 32. That in all cases of distraint and sale of goods and chattels for non-payment of taxes, provided for in this act, the bill of sale of such goods or chattels given by the officer making such sale to the purchaser thereof shall be *prima facie* evidence of the right of the officer to make such sale, and of the correctness of his proceedings in selling the same.

REDEMPTION OF LANDS SOLD FOR TAXES. COLLECTORS TO PAY FIVE PER CENT. ON MONIES HELD OVER.

SEC. 33. That when land or other real property has been redeemed by the owner, his heirs, executors or administrators, or any one for him or them, in accordance with the foregoing provisions of this act, the collectors shall, on application, pay to the purchasers the monies thus paid for their use.

Collectors to pay purchasers of land sold for taxes, amounts paid in redemption thereof, etc.

SEC. 34. Each collector shall be charged with an interest of five per cent. per month, for all monies retained in his possession beyond the time at which he is required to pay over the same by law or by regulations established by the Secretary of the Treasury, or the commissioner of taxes, under his direction.

Collectors charged five per cent. per month for monies retained.

RULES AND REGULATIONS.

SEC. 35. That the commissioner of taxes, under the direction of the Secretary of the Treasury, is authorized to establish all rules and regulations suitable and proper to carry this act into effect, which regulations shall be binding on all officers; he may in like manner, frame instructions as to all details, which shall be obligatory upon all parties embraced within the provisions of this act, and in cases where the time fixed for the performance and completion of the various duties prescribed for the various tax officers named in this act shall, from unavoidable exigencies, be insufficient, the commissioner of taxes, by authority of the Secretary of the Treasury, shall have power to make extension thereof, as circumstances and the public interest may require. And that in those States and localities, which are or may be temporarily inaccessible, or which are so remote from the seat of government, as to render it impracticable for lists or returns to be made by the time required by the provisions of this act, it shall be the duty of the commissioner of taxes, by the authority of the Secretary of the Treasury, to make such extension of the time for making such lists and returns as circumstances and the public interests may require.

Commissioner of taxes to establish rules and regulations.

To frame instructions.

To extend time allowed for performance of duties when the same is found to be insufficient.

To make extension of time in certain cases.

COMPENSATION OF DISTRICT COLLECTORS. LIEN TO ATTACH FROM DATE OF ASSESSMENT.

SEC. 36. That the compensation of district tax collectors shall be five per centum on the first twenty thousand dollars collected and paid over, and two and a half per centum on all sums beyond that amount collected and paid over, until such compensation shall attain a maximum of two thousand dollars. And there shall be allowed and paid to the several assessors for their services under this act, five dollars for every day employed in making lists and assessments under this act, the number of days being certified by the district collector and approved by the State collector, and also five dollars for every hundred taxable persons contained in the list as completed by such assessor and delivered to the collector: *Provided*, such compensation shall not exceed one thousand dollars.

Maximum compensation of district collectors.

Compensation of assessors.

Maximum compensation of assessors.

SEC. 37. The lien for the tax shall attach from the date of assessment, and shall follow the property into every State of this Confederacy; and in case any person shall attempt to remove any property, which may be liable to tax, beyond the jurisdiction of the State in which the tax is payable, without payment of the tax, the collector of the district may distrain upon and sell the same in the manner as is provided in cases where default is made in the payment of the tax.

Lien for tax to attach from date of assessment and to follow property.

Collector may distrain and sell property about to be moved without payment of tax.

DISBURSING CLERK FOR OFFICE OF COMMISSIONER OF TAXES.

SEC. 38. That the Secretary of the Treasury shall appoint a disbursing clerk for the office of commissioner of taxes, who shall give bond with sureties faithfully to discharge the duties of his office, in such amount as may be prescribed by the Secretary of the Treasury, and shall receive, in compensation therefor, the sum of seventeen hundred and fifty dollars. And it shall be the duty of said disbursing clerk to

Disbursing clerk to give bond.

Compensation.

Duties.

examine and settle all accounts for salaries, commissions, and other expenses incidental to the assessment and collection of the taxes provided for by law, and he shall render monthly or quarterly statements to the proper auditor, as shall be directed by the Secretary of the Treasury, and shall conduct the correspondence in relation thereto, under the supervision and control of the commissioner of taxes.

PERSONS ELIGIBLE TO OFFICE UNDER THE ACT.

SEC. 39. No person shall be eligible to fill any of the offices enumerated in this act, unless he shall have attained the age of forty years, or, if under that age, shall have been discharged from military duty, by reason of disabilities received in the military service, or shall have been declared unfit for military duty, by the proper board, from other causes.

MISCELLANEOUS PROVISIONS.

Appointment of officers may be made by President during recess of Senate.

Such appointments to be submitted at next session.

To expire in case they are not confirmed.

SEC. 40. That all the officers mentioned in this act, whose appointments are required to be made by and with the advice and consent of the Senate, may be appointed by the President during the recess of the Senate, and said appointments shall be submitted to the Senate for confirmation at its next session, and in case the same be not confirmed by the Senate at said session, such appointments shall expire at the end of the session.

Act not to alter, impair or repeal, the tax act.

SEC. 41. That the provisions of this act shall not be construed to alter, impair, or repeal any portion of the act passed at the present session entitled "An Act to lay taxes for the common defence and carry on the government of the Confederate States," regulating the manner of ascertaining and assessing the income tax for the year eighteen hundred and sixty-three, and for subsequent years, and the manner of ascertaining, assessing and collecting the tax in kind: *Provided*, That all valuations required in ascertaining and assessing the said income tax and tax in kind, shall be made in Confederate notes.

Valuations of assessments to be made in Confederate notes.

Tax-payer allowed to make pre-payments of taxes and entitled to interest thereon.

Certificate thereof not transferable.

SEC. 42. That the Secretary of the Treasury may prescribe regulations to enable any tax-payer to pay into the treasury, in advance such sum as he may choose on account of taxes to accrue against him, and to obtain therefor a certificate bearing interest at the rate of five per cent. a year until his taxes are payable, but such certificate shall not be transferable.

All bonds made payable to Confederate States.

SEC. 43. All bonds required to be executed under the provisions of this act shall be made payable to the Confederate States.

Valuation of credits.

SEC. 44. In no valuation of credits under the provisions of this act, shall any credit upon which the holder will endorse in writing his willingness to receive Confederate notes in payment, be valued at a higher rate.

APPROVED May 1st, 1863.

AN ACT TO AMEND THE ASSESSMENT ACT.

Feby. 17. 1864

AN ACT to amend the "Act for the Assessment and Collection of Taxes," approved May first, eighteen hundred and sixty-three.

The Congress of the Confederate States of America do enact, That the "Act for the Assessment and Collection of Taxes," approved May first, eighteen hundred and sixty-three, is hereby amended as follows: I. The Secretary of the Treasury is hereby authorized to appoint a Chief Clerk for the office of the Commissioner of Taxes, who shall receive the same compensation allowed by law to the chief clerks of the other bureaus in the Treasury Department. II. The second section of the said act is hereby amended and re-enacted so as to read as follows:

Section 2. That for the purpose of assessing, levying and collecting all taxes and internal duties, each State shall constitute a tax division over which shall be appointed by the President, with the advice and consent of the Senate, one State Collector, who shall be a resident and freeholder in such State, with a salary of one tenth of one per cent. on the amount collected in each State. *Provided,* That in no case, shall the salary be less than two thousand nor more than five thousand dollars, and said State Collector shall, under the regulations prescribed by the Commissioner of Taxes, under the direction of the Secretary of the Treasury, be charged with the duties imposed upon himself, and with the superintendence and direction of all the duties of the various officers in his division or State, created by this act. The said State Collector shall give bond with sureties, to discharge the duties of his office in such amount as may be prescribed by the Secretary of the Treasury, and shall take oath faithfully to discharge the duties of his office, and to support and defend the Constitution of the Confederate States.

Third. Thirteenth section of the said act is hereby amended and re-enacted so as to read as follows:

Section 13. That the lists aforesaid shall be taken at such times as may be prescribed by the Commissioner of Taxes, under the direction of the Secretary of the Treasury, or with reference to the time when the said taxes become due, and the assessors respectively after collecting the said lists, shall proceed to arrange the same, and to make two general lists, the first of which shall exhibit in alphabetical order the names of all persons liable to pay any tax, residing within the collection district, together with the value and assessment or enumeration, as the case may require, of the objects liable to taxation within such district, for which each such person is liable, or for which any firm, company or corporation is liable, with the amount of tax payable thereon; and the second list shall exhibit in alphabetical order, the names of all persons residing out of the collection district, owners of property, within the district, together with the value and assessment, or enumeration thereof, as the case may be, with the amount of tax payable thereon as aforesaid. The forms of said general lists, shall be devised and prescribed by the State Collector, under the direction of the Commissioner of Taxes; and lists taken according to such forms, shall be made out by the assessor or assessors, and delivered to the district collector within thirty days after the time fixed by this act as aforesaid, and if any assessor shall fail to perform any duty assigned by this act, within the time aforesaid, not being prevented therefrom by sickness or other unavoidable cause, every such assessor shall be discharged from office, and shall moreover forfeit and pay the sum of two hundred dollars, to be recovered for the use of the Confederate States, with cost of suit.

Fourth. The twenty-fourth section of said act is hereby amended and re-enacted so as to read as follows:

"Section 24. That all property, coin, currency, credits, income and profits, and every article or object subjected to taxation shall be estimated, valued, and assessed at the value thereof at the time of assessment, in Confederate Treasury notes unless otherwise provided in the law imposing the tax."

Fifth. The thirty-sixth section of the said act is hereby amended and re-enacted so as to read as follows:

"Section 36. The compensation of district tax collectors, shall be five per cent. on the first twenty thousand dollars, collected and paid over, two per cent. on the next thirty thousand dollars collected and paid over, one per cent. on the next fifty thousand dollars collected and paid over and one-tenth of one per cent. on all monies collected and paid over above the sum of one hundred thousand dollars, and there shall be allowed and paid to the several assessors for their services under this act, eight dollars for every day employed in making lists and assessments under this act, the number of days being certified by the district collector and approved by the State Collector, and also eight dollars for every hundred taxable persons contained in the list as completed by such assessor and delivered to the collector: *Provided*, That in cities and large towns, when in his judgment the public interest may require it, the Secretary of the Treasury shall have power to increase the per diem compensation of assessors, not to exceed ten dollars per day."

Section 2. Referees under the "act to lay taxes for the common defence and carry on the Government of the Confederate States," approved April twenty-fourth, eighteen hundred and sixty-three, shall be paid for their services five dollars a day, while so employed, and assessors and collectors shall have power to compel the attendance of witnesses, by written summons, and to require their testimony in any matter or investigation, in reference to the assessments and estimates of taxes; such witnesses shall be entitled to the same compensation allowed witnesses for attending upon Courts of record in the State where they may be required to attend. Payments to referees and witnesses, shall be made by the disbursing clerk, in the office of the Commissioner of Taxes, upon accounts certified as shall be required by the regulations of said office.

Section 3. When personal chattels or goods distrained for taxes, shall be claimed by any person other than the party for whose default the distraint is made, the claimant shall file with the officer making the distraint, an affidavit, stating distinctly the nature and extent of his claim; and thereupon the right of property shall be determined as follows: The collector and the claimant shall each select a disinterested freeholder of the vicinage, who may call in a third, in case of disagreement. If the claimant shall neglect or refuse to select a freeholder on his part, the Collector may select two, who shall proceed as before provided. Witnesses may be introduced by either party, and the decision in each case shall be final and conclusive. The referees and witnesses in such cases, shall be paid as provided in the second section, and any witness failing to attend upon the summons of referees, in any case mentioned in this act, shall be subject to a penalty of one hundred dollars, to be recovered with costs, in any court of competent jurisdiction.

Section 4. The Secretary of the Treasury is hereby authorized to dispense with the use of individual lists, bills; or statements required of tax-payers under the provisions of the "Act to lay taxes for the common defence and carry on the Government of the Confederate States," approved April twenty-fourth, eighteen hundred and sixty-three, and the "Act for the assessment and collection of taxes," approved May first, eighteen hundred and sixty-three, and the Commissionissioner of Taxes is hereby authorized and required under the direction of the Secretary of the Treasury, to devise the manner and form of making returns and estimates of taxes, and to establish such system as may be deemed best for the assessment and collection of the taxes, without the individual lists, bills or statements aforesaid; *Provided*, That the estimates of referees shall be made as heretofore, in accordance with the provisions of the acts aforesaid.

Section 5. If the Treasurer, or Assistant Treasurer, or depositary of money of the Confederate States, or any clerk in the office of such treasurer, assistant treasurer, or depository, or any collector of taxes, shall prior to the first day of January, eighteen hundred and sixty-four, in the course of the lawful business of such officer, have received in payment or on deposit in such office, any forged or counterfeit treasury notes, and shall establish by proof to the satisfaction of the Secretary of the Treasury, that the receipt of such forged or counterfeit treasury notes, was not the result of any want of diligence or care, and attention, on the part of such officer, but was in good faith a mistake, involving no fault on his part, said Secretary shall have power to relieve such officer from liability, on account of any forged or counterfeit note so received.

Approved February 17th, 1864.

INDEX.

www.ingramcontent.com/pod-product-compliance
Lightning Source LLC
Chambersburg PA
CBHW031800090426
42739CB00008B/1098
9783337714970